Learning and Tea
Practical Skills

As seen on TV

POST-16 LEARNING

ACKNOWLEDGEMENTS

The authors wish to thank all the students, teacher trainees, colleagues, family and friends who have contributed to this book, either directly or indirectly. Thanks in particular to those who recommended TV programmes we might otherwise not have watched.

To order our books please go to our website www.criticalpublishing.com or contact our distributor Ingram Publisher Services, telephone 01752 202301 or email IPSUK.orders@ingramcontent.com. Details of bulk order discounts can be found at www.criticalpublishing.com/delivery-information.

Our titles are also available in electronic format: for individual use via our website and for libraries and other institutions from all the major ebook platforms.

Learning and Teaching
Practical Skills

As seen on TV

**ANDREW ARMITAGE
AND HARRIET HARPER**

POST-16 LEARNING

First published in 2024 by Critical Publishing Ltd

All rights reserved. No part of this publication may be reproduced, stored in a retrieval system, or transmitted in any form or by any means, electronic, mechanical, photocopying, recording or otherwise, without prior permission in writing from the publisher.

The authors have made every effort to ensure the accuracy of information contained in this publication, but assume no responsibility for any errors, inaccuracies, inconsistencies and omissions. Likewise, every effort has been made to contact copyright holders. If any copyright material has been reproduced unwittingly and without permission the Publisher will gladly receive information enabling them to rectify any error or omission in subsequent editions.

Copyright © 2024 Andrew Armitage and Harriet Harper

British Library Cataloguing in Publication Data
A CIP record for this book is available from the British Library

ISBN: 978-1-915713-66-7

This book is also available in the following e-book formats:
EPUB ISBN: 978-1-915713-67-4
Adobe e-book ISBN: 978-1-915713-68-1

The rights of Andrew Armitage and Harriet Harper to be identified as the Authors of this work have been asserted by them in accordance with the Copyright, Design and Patents Act 1988.

Text design by Greensplash
Cover design by Out of House Limited
Project Management by Newgen Publishing UK

Critical Publishing
3 Connaught Road
St Albans
AL3 5RX

www.criticalpublishing.com

Endorsements

Another ITE textbook? This not just 'another' book, it's the first of its kind. The one real standout feature of the book is the use of comparisons to TV shows. This innovative approach allows trainees to connect with some challenging and abstract concepts in concrete terms – and they can then always look to YouTube for clips of the shows.

The book covers a wide range of topics, all relevant to the post-compulsory sector. The content is presented in a clear and accessible manner, like listening to a great teacher or mentor, who has walked the walk, gained their battle scars and become a better and stronger practitioner as a result.

The book reflects the evolving landscape of post-compulsory education and incorporates the latest research. The reflective tasks prompt the reader to engage with the material and apply it to their own teaching contexts.

What a super book – comprehensive coverage, practical approaches, and meaningful application. A must-have text for trainee teachers, subject mentors, and ITE teachers alike.

Dr Clare Winder
Initial Teacher Education
University of Central Lancashire

This text is a unique, and quirky, blend of learning and teaching and the rise of reality TV shows. Regardless of the reader's feelings about reality TV, there is no escaping the link between the programme and its contestants and the learner in the FE and Skills classroom. The examples of how people learn, and the benefits of real-world learning are cleverly interwoven into the text with snippets from some of the post popular programmes on TV. Any trainee teacher, or indeed any teacher, cannot fail to see the connection and use some of the suggestions to enhance their own practice. An engaging read.

Dr Lynn Senior
Consortium Director
University of Huddersfield

Skills competitions are a major feature of TV schedules with many very popular and long-running shows. They speak to our interest in seeing people develop their skill and confidence through practice and hard work, often against the odds. We love to follow the challenges faced by participants as well as their joy and satisfaction as they master a craft. Sharing other people's learning journeys can help us understand how we learn as well as inspiring and motivating us.

This highly original book from Harriet Harper and Andy Armitage draws on TV skills shows to provide useful practical advice for teachers on how to develop their students' skills, confidence, mastery and fluency. It will be an excellent resource for any teacher seeking to improve their professional practice.

Eddie Playfair
Senior Policy Manager
Association of Colleges

The authors ask their readers, in the course of their book, to use (popular TV) programmes as their own teaching resources, to use them to reflect on their practice, as illustrations of educational theory, as examples of assessment or judgement (good or bad) or as examples of strategies or scenarios for planning teaching and learning. This innovative and lively training text enables them superbly to do all of the above.

Dr Alison Cogger
Principal Lecturer, Initial Teacher Education
Canterbury Christ Church University

I love the premise of this book: that TV programmes such as Strictly Come Dancing *and* The Great British Bake Off *play a similar role to further education – they develop people's skills. The authors draw on insightful examples from popular programmes like* The Great British Sewing Bee *and* Dragons' Den *which focus on teaching and assessing skills. So simple and so powerful.*

Unlike many books on teaching and learning in the FE and Skills sector, theoretical concepts are clearly explained as you read, so teachers, trainees and teacher educators could find themselves re-thinking the activities they design, the models they follow and the examples they use. There's no separate chapter for 'theory', thank goodness. I so wish I'd had this book when I first started as a lecturer in the FE and Skills sector. It has made me think differently about my own teaching. And it's a joy to read.

Dr Rebecca Eliahoo, SFHEA
WEA tutor

Three cheers for Andrew Armitage and Harriet Harper! As teacher trainers and educators, we all encourage our student-teachers – whether in their initial training or as part of continuing professional development – to keep in mind the importance of two key principles: the need to engage learners by using something familiar to them as a starting point; and the role that novelty and fun play in keeping that engagement going. This timely book, by drawing analogies with the learning models evident on reality tv shows, combines these two principles. It provides an effective – and at the same time entertaining – way in to discussions of key issues and theoretical models. The novelty of this approach is bound to be a powerful motivating factor in the learning of teachers themselves, while at the same time modelling for them the importance of building familiar starting points and enjoyment into their own planning and practice.

Susan Wallace,
Emerita Professor of Education,
Nottingham Trent University

The book would be a very useful introduction for Further Education Teachers studying a teaching qualification or simply wanting to find out more about the sector and their work. It is written in an engaging and readable style and is clearly informed by a great deal of experience in the sector. The reference to reality TV programmes adds novelty value, and also helps to anchor the book in real-world experience. While these are UK programmes, they would be comprehensible to readers in any country.

Professor Erica Smith,
Emerita Professor (Vocational Education and Training)
Federation University Australia

Contents

Meet the authors   *viii*

1. The further education contexts, the students and teachers, and the TV programmes   1
2. Learning   18
3. Teaching   36
4. Assessment   54
5. Inclusion, diversity and well-being   77
6. Education for sustainable development   95
7. Expertise, professional development and a spot, swot and plot   116

TV programmes   *133*

Index   *135*

Meet the authors

Harriet Harper has held a variety of teaching and management roles in further education and higher education. She was a teacher educator at the University of Greenwich for seven years and as one of His Majesty's Inspectors for ten years she specialised in further education and teacher training. Now she combines a number of professional freelance activities as a teacher, critical friend, college governor, researcher and author. She is a Principal Fellow of the Higher Education Academy and author of *Outstanding Teaching in Lifelong Learning*.

Andy Armitage was head of the Department of Post-Compulsory Education at Canterbury Christ Church University and taught in secondary, further, adult and community, and higher education for over 40 years. He was an associate inspector and then Ofsted inspector from 2011 to 2015. He now works as a consultant with universities, advising them on teacher training, and as a staff developer in the education and training sector. As Chair of the Universities' Council for the Education of Teachers Post-16 Committee from 2014 to 2017, he was closely involved with the development of the education and training apprenticeships. He is co-author of a number of key texts for further education ITE programmes.

The further education contexts, the students and teachers, and the TV programmes

1.1 INTRODUCTION

This introduction to the chapter sets out the rationale for our approach to the book as a whole, using TV programmes as stimuli for the teaching and learning activities of those training to teach in the further education (FE) sector. Section 1.2 looks firstly at the contexts in which FE operates and the key learning institutions/providers. This is followed by an outline of the major qualification types and curriculum changes. Next, section 1.3 considers the range of students in the sector, while section 1.4 examines the key features and roles of the FE workforce. In section 1.5 we list the main TV programme types, while section 1.6 explains the methodology and how to use the book. The final section, 1.7, sets out the key issues addressed in future chapters.

The seed for this book was sown by a comparison one of the authors made between the nature of TV programmes such as *Strictly Come Dancing* and the role FE plays in developing the skills of its students (Harper, 2022). In both, participants embark on a learning journey; there is inclusion with high expectations of all, regardless of any specific (dis)ability; good teaching is key, as is formative feedback; and participants are socialised into their respective disciplines, acquiring technical skills. Of course, there are important differences between FE and the TV medium. Arguably, one of the most important is resourcing:

> *Money matters. In* Strictly, *a contestant's payment increases the longer they stay in the competition and the tabloids report huge payments for professionals and judges. Also, there are dozens of people behind the scenes, as there are in further education (FE) and training. It would be useful to compare money spent per contestant on* Strictly *to funding allocation per student in FE. Finance makes a significant difference to what can be achieved.*
>
> (Harper, 2022)

Despite this mismatch, there is no doubt that both FE and TV have a significant influence over the population. According to Ofcom, UK video viewing per person (via all methods and devices) was four hours and 28 minutes per day in 2022. Recent research by the Education and Training Foundation (ETF) and the Society for Education and Training (SET) reported the following.

> *A survey of 2,000 UK adults found that the majority have witnessed the transformative power of FE and Training in some way. Two-fifths (40%) have taken part in some type of FE and Training themselves and 56% know someone who has. Almost 9 in 10 (88%) of those with a friend, family member or colleague who's taken part in FE and Training found it to be a positive step for that person in developing their career.*
>
> (ETF/SET, 2021)

John Reith's concept of broadcasting informed not just the BBC but similar organisations around the world. He worked in the 1920s for the British Broadcasting Company Ltd (now the BBC) and established the tradition of independent public service broadcasting, focusing on three key aims: informing, educating and entertaining. At first sight, popular TV might seem an unlikely area for trainee teachers to focus on since it appears to fulfil only the last of the Reithian aims. However, in recent years, the number of popular TV programmes addressing the first two aims has grown dramatically.

In some respects, the book draws on cultivation theory, a set of sociological and communication theories established by George Gerbner in the 1970s (Morgan, 2002). The central tenet of these theories is that the longer viewers spend watching TV, the greater the effect this has on their perception of the real world. Students, and indeed teachers, may well be affected by what they watch and how long they spend absorbed in reality TV programmes. This may have an impact on students' approach to learning, their motivation and their aspirations. However, our book focuses less on the impact of TV on viewers in general and more on how we can use TV for trainee teachers to reflect on, and evaluate, different approaches to teaching, learning and assessment.

Our interest lies particularly in the connections between TV and lifelong learning. Certain types of reality TV programmes allow viewers to see how untrained beginners, with hard work, motivation and the support of an experienced professional, can challenge themselves, perform to an impressive standard or produce something of a high quality. If viewers are watching programmes about how to bake, garden, cook, sing, sew, dance, throw pots, skate or restore antiques, to what extent is this encouraging them to develop further their own knowledge and skills? What can trainee teachers learn from the teaching, learning and assessment they observe in these programmes?

In X (formerly Twitter) the journalist and Channel 4 news presenter Krishnan Guru-Murthy, when voted off in *Strictly Come Dancing*, wrote:

> *That's all folks. Heartbroken. Thanks for the love and support – I'm so delighted that so many people enjoyed watching us. Strictly brought me more happiness than I ever imagined. It has been life changing and life affirming. There is something about taking big risks, performing, giving it everything, making yourself totally vulnerable and shedding the armour you normally use to survive that is exhilarating, liberating and inspiring. Dancing is physically and emotionally unique. I owe the vast majority of it to my stunning dance partner.*
>
> (Guru-Murthy, 12 November 2023)

Given that this very positive reflection on his experience quickly received 1.4 million views and over 900 re-posts, it is safe to assume that it may well have encouraged others to try their hand at a new skill, change their lives in some way or even enrol on an adult education course.

Guru-Murthy is not alone in describing his experience as life changing and life affirming, or in emphasising how critical his teacher was to his success. Other former contestants have made similar observations and, in interviews, on social media and spin-off programmes, they also comment on their 'new family', the fellow contestants who have become friends. The camaraderie and strong social bonds that develop between contestants on these shows highlight the value of group cohesion and peer support. Socially situated learning, when people learn together collectively, is explored in Chapter 2.

Whether it is a programme about developing skills, creating a masterpiece, dating or following people's daily lives, most of these shows tell the stories of developing relationships. Part of the attraction for viewers is that they can experience vicariously the various emotional rollercoasters and in doing so they reflect on their own lives.

Wendy Horrex highlights the importance of storytelling in the training and development of FE teachers:

> *For a student or new teacher, the telling of stories to peers, tutors and mentors can help to master this skill so they can use it in their own classroom to build relationships with learners and bring meaning and application of wider principles that they are teaching. Opportunities to practise this skill in the teacher education classroom can prepare student teachers for using it effectively in their own classroom.*
>
> (Horrex, 2023)

Task

- Consider an event/incident in your own teaching which illustrates a key point for you about FE teaching you think you could usefully relate to your peer trainees.
- Alternatively, consider an event/incident in your pre-teaching working life or your education experience which you might usefully relate to your students.

Often in these programmes, 'ordinary' people are brought together in a single place, for example, another country, a house, a kitchen, a hotel or even a jungle. This is because the drama of the programme is largely driven by people's relationships with each other when they are under pressure.

When teachers and students leave the classroom for other learning venues, there is often a transformation through their experiences. Teachers' relationships with students often change dramatically in non-classroom contexts, as do students' relationships with one another. Students who perform less well in traditional classrooms may develop skills and abilities they never knew they had. This can be particularly true of work experience or in a particular context which builds personal skills and qualities, such as quick thinking, resourcefulness and resilience, for example. These venues need not necessarily be outside the college: many colleges will have hair salons, construction workshops and restaurants, for example, in which students can learn and work.

Task

- Choose a non-classroom venue or experience which might be a useful teaching and learning resource in your subject area. This could be within college or outside, such as a work venue, a community venue, art gallery, museum, place of historical interest, leisure centre, farm or hospital.
- Plan the visit, including any preparatory and follow-up work, and clarify the specific educational benefits of the visit.

Many of the most popular reality shows have a 'celebrity' version, for example: *Celebrity MasterChef* and *Who Wants to Be a Millionaire? Celebrity Special*. The attraction here, apart from the obvious draw of celebrity, is that it is unlikely that the celebrity's fame is connected with the skills they need to demonstrate in the programme and therefore the outcome of the competition remains unpredictable, and the show is dramatic as a result.

Of course, to ensure drama, all of these programmes, whether they involve celebrities or 'ordinary' people, are edited and staged. Hence, authentic learning situations are not portrayed realistically. In effect, reality TV is a *'mediated reality'* (Cato and Carpentier, 2010) where scenes are manipulated and exaggerated for entertainment purposes and to increase ratings. Denby (2021) notes that while, for this reason, programmes like *Love Island* are not entirely authentic, contestants do display real-life attitudes and emotions and so it is a way to capture societal attitudes. Her research into episodes of *Love Island* as a case study concludes that despite a shift towards greater gender equality, traditional gendered ideals continue to exist in heterosexual relationships, which disadvantages women.

Reality TV programmes do not operate within a socio-political vacuum. The connections between these programmes, society and teaching and learning are complex and controversial. In an analysis of reality TV, Windle (2010) argues that:

> ... reality television talent-quest formats model the normative neoliberal worker and learner – roles which are increasingly drawn together. In the age of 'life-long learning' and shifting employment demands, new models of the supple, adaptable and willing learner are increasingly important both to meeting neoliberal economic demands and to legitimating them. As they appear in reality television, these models stand as ideological exemplars for the management of disappointment, the cultivation of hope and the maintenance of belief in meritocracy. Compliance,

effort, just desserts and luck are emphasized in programs that offer viewers self-narratives that allow them to account for both their own circumstances and wider inequalities. As a vehicle of public pedagogy, reality television plays a central role in defining the place of learning in neoliberal self-actualization.

(Windle, 2010, p 251)

Regardless of views on the impact of reality TV on society, these shows, given their popularity, provide a useful starting point for discussion within the context of teacher education. While the book focuses primarily on those programmes that involve some aspect of learning and also on positive examples, this does not in any way reflect a lack of awareness of educationally unsound practice or negative stereotypes. Voting off and evicting contestants, for example, is cruel and not used in teaching for good reasons, while excessive rewards for winning, even if desired, are not an option in an educational setting.

The fact that programmes like *Love Island* promote unrealistic ideals of human beauty and perpetuate sexist attitudes to women makes them an ideal resource to use with students to discuss issues such as self-esteem and gender equality, and to deepen students' critical thinking. Similarly, *The Undateables*, which follows a group of people living with challenging conditions in their attempts to find love, can be used to provoke thinking about the portrayal on TV of people with disabilities. Views as to whether or not it is an exploitative approach may well differ and therefore promote rich debate. Issues around diversity are explored further in Chapter 5.

1.2 THE CONTEXTS

Further education providers

There are 228 FE colleges in England.

- *Colleges prepare 1.6 million students with valuable skills.*
- *91% of colleges were judged good or outstanding for overall effectiveness at their most recent Ofsted inspection.*
- *124,000 16 to 18-year-olds students in colleges are doing A Level courses.*
- *549,000 students in colleges are taking STEM subjects.*
- *179,000 students in colleges retake GCSE English and/or maths.*

(Association of Colleges, 2023)

General further education (GFE) colleges have students who are over the age of 16, although many cater for 14–16 year olds from local schools who come into college for (mainly vocational) link courses. GFE colleges have a wide range of students who are studying on both a full- and part-time basis. In Sixth Form Colleges students are more likely to be 16–19 and studying academic courses on a full-time basis and around two thirds of them progress to higher education. Land-based colleges provide education and training in areas relating to animals, plants, farming and the environment. Art, design and performance art colleges offer courses in subjects such as fine art, graphic design, jewellery design and performing arts, including dance and ballet. National specialist colleges (also known as independent specialist colleges) offer specialist support to young people with learning difficulties and/or disabilities.

Independent training/learning providers now make a major contribution to post-16 learning nationally. Between August 2022 and April 2023, 27 per cent of all FE and skills enrolments were with an independent training provider. In addition to FE and skills provision, independent training providers offer the following provision: apprenticeships, skills boot camps, adult education, 16–19 study programmes, support for those not in employment, education or training (NEET), vocational qualifications, employability skills, offender learning, and work and health programmes (Association of Employment and Learning Providers, 2023).

There are over 200 adult community education providers delivering adult education through a network of centres in almost every city and town, with learning often taking place in a variety of community settings.

Despite its criticality for rehabilitation and eventual reintegration of offenders into society, prison education is a neglected area of FE. Provision is varied in quality and quantity across the secure estate.

Task

- Write a one-page introduction to the institution you teach in, describing its key features such as campus buildings/settings and range of subjects offered, including institutional specialisms. Draw on the institution's website and, if possible, strategic plan.

With regard to post-16 funding:

> *… aside from inflationary pressures, colleges and sixth forms are facing three other challenges. First, the number of 16- and 17-year-olds is rising rapidly as a result of a population boom moving through the education system. Second, the impact of the pandemic remains significant, with changes in young people's education decisions and the effects of lost learning. Third, the government is overhauling the post-16 qualification landscape, which means that many providers are having to change the courses they offer students.*
>
> (Institute for Fiscal Studies, 2022)

The Association of Colleges (2023) explains income sources for FE as follows:

- *the largest proportion, 55% comes from 16–18 education;*
- *adult education 13%;*
- *apprenticeships 7%;*

- higher education 7%;
- grants 7%;
- fees 4%;
- commercial 3%;
- other 4%.

Task

- There will be a senior manager responsible for funding in your institution. Find out who they are and ask them to share with you the institution's major funding challenges now and in the future.

Qualifications and curricula

Most qualifications have a level of difficulty. The higher the level, the more difficult the qualification. The Regulated Qualifications Framework for England, Wales and Northern Ireland has nine qualification levels, as shown in Table 1.1.

Table 1.1 Regulated Qualifications Framework

Entry level	Level 1	Level 2
Each entry level qualification is available at three sub-levels – 1, 2 and 3. Entry level 3 is the most difficult. Entry level qualifications are: • entry level award; • entry level certificate (ELC); • entry level diploma; • entry level English for speakers of other languages (ESOL); • entry level essential skills; • entry level functional skills; • Skills for Life.	Level 1 qualifications are: • first certificate; • GCSE – grades 3, 2, 1 or grades D, E, F, G; • level 1 award; • level 1 certificate; • level 1 diploma; • level 1 ESOL; • level 1 essential skills; • level 1 functional skills; • level 1 national vocational qualification (NVQ); • music grades 1, 2 and 3.	Level 2 qualifications are: • CSE – grade 1; • GCSE – grades 9, 8, 7, 6, 5, 4 or grades A*, A, B, C; • intermediate apprenticeship; • level 2 award; • level 2 certificate; • level 2 diploma; • level 2 ESOL; • level 2 essential skills; • level 2 functional skills; • level 2 national certificate; • level 2 national diploma; • level 2 NVQ; • music grades 4 and 5; • O level – grade A, B or C.

Level 3	Level 4	Level 5
Level 3 qualifications are: - A level; - access to higher education diploma; - advanced apprenticeship; - applied general; - AS level; - international Baccalaureate diploma; - level 3 award; - level 3 certificate; - level 3 diploma; - level 3 ESOL; - level 3 national certificate; - level 3 national diploma; - level 3 NVQ; - music grades 6, 7 and 8; - tech level; - T levels.	Level 4 qualifications are: - certificate of higher education (Cert HE); - higher apprenticeship; - higher national certificate (HNC); - level 4 award; - level 4 certificate; - level 4 diploma; - level 4 NVQ.	Level 5 qualifications are: - diploma of higher education (DipHE); - foundation degree; - higher national diploma (HND); - level 5 award; - level 5 certificate; - level 5 diploma; - level 5 NVQ.
Level 6	**Level 7**	**Level 8**
Level 6 qualifications are: - degree apprenticeship; - degree with honours – for example bachelor of the arts (BA) hons, bachelor of science (BSc) hons; - graduate certificate; - graduate diploma; - level 6 award; - level 6 certificate; - level 6 diploma; - level 6 NVQ; - ordinary degree without honours.	Level 7 qualifications are: - integrated master's degree, for example master of engineering (MEng); - level 7 award; - level 7 certificate; - level 7 diploma; - level 7 NVQ; - master's degree, for example master of arts (MA), master of science (MSc); - postgraduate certificate; - postgraduate certificate in education (PGCE); - postgraduate diploma.	Level 8 qualifications are: - doctorate, for example doctor of philosophy (PhD or DPhil); - level 8 award; - level 8 certificate; - level 8 diploma.

(Ofqual, 2023)

Full-time provision for younger students

Students aged 16–19 in FE are usually working towards: a main qualification, either vocational or academic; work experience, which can take various forms such as work placements, participation in social action or volunteering; English and mathematics (students who do not have a grade 4 or above in either GCSE English or GCSE mathematics (or equivalent) continue these subjects as part of their study programme); non-qualification activity – these are activities to develop confidence and/or life skills, which may involve participating in group work, tutorials or seminars; progression support to achieve future goals will be provided, whether continuing in education or seeking employment.

Apprenticeships

Apprentices are paid employees who complete their experience in a specific occupation in one to two years. Apprentices follow specific occupational routes and they have to work for at least 30 hours per week and complete a formal period of off-the-job-training for around 20 per cent of their time. On completion of their apprenticeship, they have to meet industry standards at a specified level by undertaking end-point assessment.

Adult provision

FE is not only a place for 16 to 19 year olds to gain qualifications. Many adults also choose to take a range of part-time, professional and undergraduate courses at FE institutions for self-development or to progress their career. For example, English for speakers of other languages (ESOL) is important for adults who were born in countries where English is not a main language. FE plays a critical role for migrants and refugees, who have valuable skills and knowledge which they can only use once they have improved their communication skills in English.

Vocational/technical qualifications

BTEC qualifications are being gradually phased out. T levels were introduced in 2020 to provide students aged 16–18 with a technical alternative to A levels. T levels are in a range of occupational routes, such as agriculture, environmental and animal care; business and administration; catering and hospitality; construction; creative and design; digital; education and early years; engineering and manufacturing; hair and beauty; health and science; legal finance and accounting; and sales, marketing and procurement. T levels include three mandatory elements: core underpinning theories, concepts and workplace skills, tailored for the chosen industry or occupation; occupationally specialist skills; and an industry placement with an employer, lasting for at least 45 days.

GCSEs

GCSEs are level 1 or 2 qualifications (depending on what grade is achieved) and are usually studied full time, taking one or two years to complete. They are assessed by exams, coursework or a combination of both. With a large number of subjects available, GCSEs provide a solid foundation for further academic and vocational study; a grade 4 in English and mathematics is a prerequisite for many jobs and courses.

As a trainee teacher, it is likely that when you completed your own GCSEs, the grading system was different. A new GCSE grade scale was introduced between 2017 and 2019, as shown in Table 1.2.

Table 1.2 New grading structure for GCSEs

GCSE grading	
New grading structure	**Old grading structure**
9	A*
8	
7	A
6	B
5	
4	C
3	D
2	E
1	F
	G
U	U

Academic qualifications

Students taking A levels usually select three, or sometimes four, subjects and normally study them full time over two years. Successful completion of A levels opens up the possibility of higher education (HE) study at college, university or online. FE offers students an alternative to school for taking A levels, or an opportunity for them to retake their A levels, or the chance to take them for the first time as an adult returning to education in later life. The International Baccalaureate (IB) is offered in some schools, primarily private schools, but rarely in FE. The IB provides students with a much broader range of subjects than A level, much like the French Baccalaureate, the German Arbitur, the Spanish Bachillerato and the Italian Maturità.

Curriculum reform

The last 20 years has seen regular reform of qualifications in the 14/16–19 sector. Much of this reform has been connected with differing views about breadth and specialisation.

Task

- To what extent are your students following a broad or specialist programme? If you consider it too narrow, what else would you include? If too broad, what would you remove and why?

Curriculum reform has concerned itself with the links between education, training and work and the importance of English and mathematics. The year 2000 saw the introduction of AS levels in an attempt to broaden at least some post-16 study. In 2004, the Tomlinson Report proposed incorporating and replacing GCSEs and A levels with a diploma. Such a diploma would have integrated academic and vocational disciplines in order to close the longstanding and problematic academic/vocational divide. This was rejected by the then Blair government and a watered-down version of vocational diplomas was introduced and subsequently abandoned in 2010.

The Wolf Report of 2011 criticised the quality of many low-level vocational qualifications and argued for a more limited role for schools with regard to vocational education. The Richard Review of 2012 recommended redefining apprenticeships, focusing on more rigorous end-point assessment and using recognised industry standards to form the basis of all apprenticeships. Richard's recommendations were accepted in full by the government and were implemented. As noted above, T levels were introduced in 2020 as the technical equivalent of A levels.

The focus of the 2021 White Paper *Skills for Jobs: Lifelong Learning for Opportunity and Growth* (Department for Education, 2021) is on developing curricula so as to strengthen links between employers and FE providers. The emphasis is on defining and meeting local skills needs. FE has always worked with employers and provided flexible programmes – full time, part time, on the job and off the job. However, with skills shortages in many occupational areas, the need to focus even more on local business needs remains challenging for FE. The sector continues to adjust its curricula to balance supply and demand, carefully assessing what local employers request, what local communities need and what students choose to study. This happens within the context of colleges' mission statements and strategic aims, and these usually include commitments to make sure that people from all walks of life and all ability levels are welcome and that they thrive.

Task

- If you could reform 14–19 education, what would you keep and what would you change? Explain the rationale for your suggestions.

Reactions to the suggestion that all students should continue to study English and mathematics until the age of 18 are mixed. Putting aside educational arguments, a key practical concern is the shortage of teachers. In fact, there is, at the time of writing, a severe shortfall in all teachers recruited for 2023, with only half the places on secondary teacher training courses filled. This shortage extends to FE, with the Department for Education acknowledging this in its allocation of bursaries for new FE teachers:

> Tax-free bursaries in four 'high priority' subjects of maths, science, engineering and computing will shoot up from £26,000 to £29,000 in 2023/24, with grants for trainees in English growing from £12,000 to £15,000. The only other subject

where a bursary is available is special educational needs and disabilities (SEND) – but the amount on offer will stay at the same level of £15,000.

Research suggests that staffing in FE has fallen by a third in the last 10 years. The vacancy rate in colleges is also said to be around eight or nine per cent currently – double what it was prior to the pandemic.

Sector leaders have called on the government to step up its efforts to attract more people to teach in FE after highlighting recruitment struggles largely caused by the fact that average FE teacher wages are around £10,000 lower than schoolteachers, with universities able to pay even more, all while many technical and vocational lecturers can earn more in their industry.

(FE Week, 2023)

Task

- There will be a senior manager responsible for the recruitment of staff in your institution. Find out who they are and ask them to share with you the institution's current position with regard to staffing and what measures they are taking to recruit and retain staff.

1.3 THE STUDENTS

According to the Association of Colleges (2023) colleges educate and train 1.6 million people. Of these, there are 913,000 adults, 611,000 16–18 year olds, with an additional 46,000 taking apprenticeships through colleges, and 8000 14–15 year olds enrolled full or part time. College students have an average age of 27. There are 110,000 HE students in colleges, with a third of those entering HE via UCAS having studied in FE.

Regarding student demographics, 23 per cent of 16–18 year olds and 24 per cent of adults are from ethnic minority backgrounds, 46 per cent of 16–18 year olds and 60 per cent of adults are female and 26 per cent of 16–18 year olds and 17 per cent of adults have learning difficulties and/or a disability. Eighteen per cent of those in colleges as against 9 per cent of those in maintained schools and academy sixth forms claimed free school meals at 15.

Apart from quantitative generalisations about students in FE, it is extremely difficult to make qualitative generalisations, as Blair observes:

> Learners sit in refectories, some in overalls, some in tabards, some in football kit, some in smart clothes, some in everyday clothes, some with books, some with nail files, some old, some young, all different. The only thing they have in common is the space they are in.

(Blair, 2009, p 93)

Indeed, anyone who has taught in the sector will know that it is this rich variety of students which makes their teaching so rewarding. The reasons this range of students is to be found in FE are closely connected with what are regarded as the roles and purposes of the sector. Smith and Duckworth (2022, p 1) outline two major perspectives in the introduction to their book. On the one hand, FE is regarded as having a key role in the development of skills, particularly vocational skills; in fact, it is seen by *'government ministers, civil servants and policy makers – as the skills development arm of the national economy'*, the authors claim. The other perspective:

> *which is opposing in many ways, arises from local contexts and from the embodied experiences of teachers and students ... It sees further and adult education as being about real people with real lives and families and communities. These people have often been badly served by our system of schooling and may feel they have been written off by a system which is driven by meritocracy and fails to address issues of inequality that can shape communities' choices or lack of choices [in] their learning trajectories.*
>
> (Smith and Duckworth, 2022, p 1)

In other words, FE is partly about social justice, which is achieved by the transformation of these students' lives. In the interests of positionality, making their own lives visible as a frame for their subsequent research, Smith and Duckworth briefly tell their own stories (pp 32 and 33) as journeys.

Task

- As a trainee teaching or intending to teach in the FE sector, you have made a commitment to a very specific vocational calling. In no more than one page, tell your own story which clarifies your learning trajectory and gives an indication of how and why you got here.

Task

- Select one of your own students who you believe is having/has had a transformative experience as a result of their learning in your institution and briefly describe their learning trajectory. A semi-structured interview using prompt questions should give you sufficient information to do this.

1.4 THE WORKFORCE

The Association of Colleges (2023) notes that there are 103,000 full-time or equivalent staff in FE with just under half of these teaching staff. Sixty-four per cent of college staff are female, with 16 per cent from ethnic minority backgrounds and 5 per cent with a learning difficulty or disability. The average age of staff is 46, as opposed to 39 in schools. 8 per cent of college CEOs and principals are from black or minority ethnic backgrounds, with female principals represented at 48 per cent as against the 40 per cent of secondary headteachers and 33 per cent of university vice-chancellors.

The subject specialisms of teaching staff are as provided in Table 1.3:

Table 1.3 Staff specialisms

	% of total
Health, public services and care	11.2%
Arts, media and publishing	10.7%
Preparation for life and work	9.7%
Engineering and manufacturing technologies	8.9%
Construction, planning and the built environment	7.5%
English (including literacy)	7.2%
Business, administration and law	7.1%
Leisure, travel and tourism	5.8%
Mathematics	5.6%
Retail and commercial enterprise	4.7%
Agriculture, horticulture and animal care	4.0%
Science	3.9%
Information and communication technology (ICT)	3.6%
Education and training	2.6%
Humanities	2.1%
Languages, literature and culture	2.1%
Social sciences	1.6%
Community development	1.1%
Family learning	0.5%

(Education and Training Foundation, 2021)

Task

- In a previous task you told the story of one of your students. In this task, select one of your colleagues, a manager and/or a member of the professional services staff, and briefly tell their stories. Semi-structured interviews using prompt questions should give you sufficient information to do this.

Task

o   As a trainee teacher, you are likely to have a mentor. Watch an episode of *Strictly Come Dancing* or *Dancing on Ice* or *The Voice*. Compare the professional's role and relationship with the contestant with your role and relationship with your mentor. What are the similarities and differences? We shall return to this issue in Chapter 3.

In Chapter 3 we consider the role of the teacher, particularly the professionalism of FE teachers and their identity as dual professionals. You will be familiarised with the *Professional Standards for Teachers and Trainers*. The relationship between these standards, the qualifications needed to teach in FE and 'occupational duties' are explained in Chapter 7.

1.5 THE TV PROGRAMMES

Table 1.4 provides an overview of the main popular programme genres used in the book. These are not rigid categories; some programmes fit into more the one genre. For many of you, this will be an opportunity to review these programmes principally as a teacher rather than simply as a viewer. We ask you, in the course of the book, to use such programmes as your own teaching resources, using them to reflect on your practice, as illustrations of educational theory, as examples of assessment or judgement (good or bad) or as examples of strategies or scenarios for planning teaching and learning.

Table 1.4 TV genres

The talent competition	Self-improvement
RuPaul's Drag Race, Strictly Come Dancing, Britain's Got Talent, Ultimate Wedding Planner, The Voice and The X Factor.	DIY SOS: The Big Build, Big Dreams, Small Spaces.
The skills competition: developing expertise and creating a 'masterpiece'	**Celebrity shows**
The Great British Bake Off, MasterChef, Strictly Come Dancing, Dancing on Ice, The Great British Sewing Bee, The Great Pottery Throw Down, The Dog Academy, The Apprentice, Glow Up: Britain's Next Make-Up Star.	Celebrity MasterChef, Celebrity Tipping Point, Dancing on Ice, I'm a Celebrity… Get Me Out of Here!, Who Wants to Be a Millionaire? Celebrity Special.
Castaway/survival/race/quest	**Knowledge competition, quiz**
Race Across the World, Freeze the Fear with Wim Hof.	Traitors, University Challenge, QI, Countdown, Who Wants to Be a Millionaire?
Dreams come true	**Following people's daily lives**
Ground Force, Your Home Made Perfect, Dragons' Den.	Love Island, The Only Way Is Essex, I'm a Celebrity… Get Me Out of Here!, Made in Chelsea.
Dating shows	**Panel games**
Love Island, The Undateables.	University Challenge, QI, Tipping Point.

1.6 METHODOLOGY

The authors are both experienced FE teachers and teacher educators. While we have drawn on literature throughout the book that will be familiar to many who teach on teacher education programmes, we have also sought to include a wider and more diverse range of sources. In watching lots of TV programmes, many of which were new to us, and reviewing research relating to the media, we have gone beyond our normal comfort zones. We have learned a lot from the process and from each other, reflecting our own commitment to lifelong learning.

Although each chapter centres around a particular topic, inevitably many themes recur and cut across those identified in the chapter headings. The book has a developmental structure and references are made in later chapters to topics discussed earlier on in the book. While some of you will want to dip into sections, we suggest that, if possible, you work through the book from beginning to the end. We recognise it may not always be possible to watch episodes or clips that are suggested, but tasks are provided in every chapter to enable you to engage in active learning by reflecting on what you read and applying it to *your* context. Where possible, if learning in a group, we recommend that you discuss your task responses with colleagues, either in person or online.

1.7 CONCLUSION

This chapter has introduced you to the rationale for our approach in the book, explaining why and how TV programmes can be used by trainee teachers. We have noted the contexts in which FE takes place as well as the key learning institutions/providers. We have considered the major qualification types and areas of curriculum change, the range of FE students in the sector, as well as the key features and roles of the FE workforce.

This book is a textbook for trainee teachers. It is not a book *about* TV. For that reason, we have chosen chapter headings to reflect what we consider to be the main themes for trainee teachers. As such, the following chapters deal with FE teachers' core business: bringing about effective learning through high-quality teaching and assessment; attending to inclusion, diversity and well-being; focusing on sustainable development; and reviewing and planning the development of their own professional practice.

REFERENCES

Association of Colleges (2023) College Key Facts. [online] Available at: www.aoc.co.uk/about/college-key-facts (accessed 11 February 2024).

Association of Employment and Learning Providers (2023) *Key Facts About Independent Training Providers*. [online] Available at: www.aelp.org.uk/media/5hpdcdlp/keyfacts-2023.pdf (accessed 11 February 2024).

Blair, E (2009) A Further Education College as a Heterotopia. *Research in Post-Compulsory Education*, 14(1): 93–101.

Cato, M and Carpentier, F (2010) Conceptualizations of Female Empowerment and Enjoyment of Sexualized Characters in Reality Television. *Mass Communication and Society*, 13(3): 270–8.

Denby, A (2021) Toxicity and Femininity in Love Island: How Reality Dating Shows Perpetuate Sexist Attitudes Towards Women. *Frontiers in Sociology*, 6.

Department for Education (2021) *Skills for Jobs: Lifelong Learning for Opportunity and Growth.* [online] Available at: https://assets.publishing.service.gov.uk/media/601980f2e90e07128a353aa3/Skills_for_jobs_lifelong_learning_for_opportunity_and_growth__web_version_.pdf (accessed 11 February 2024).

Education and Training Foundation (ETF) (2021) *So What Is the FE Sector? A Guide to the Further Education System in England.* London: Education and Training Foundation.

Education and Training Foundation/Society for Education and Training (ETF/SET) (2021) Together We Transform. [online] Available at: www.et-foundation.co.uk/together-we-transform (accessed 11 February 2024).

FE Week (2023) DfE Hikes FE Teacher Training Bursaries. [online] Available at: https://feweek.co.uk/dfe-hikes-fe-teacher-training-bursaries (accessed 11 February 2024).

Guru-Murthy, K (2023). [online] Available at: https://twitter.com/krishgm/status/1723792075156529187 (accessed 11 February 2024).

Harper, H (2022) Up the Leaderboard. *InTuition*, Winter 2022. London: ETF/SET.

Horrex, W (2023) Time for a Story. *InTuition*, Issue 53, Autumn 2023. London: ETF/SET.

Institute for Fiscal Studies (2022) Further Education and Skills. [online] Available at: https://ifs.org.uk/education-spending/further-education-and-skills (accessed 11 February 2024).

Morgan, M (ed) (2002) *Against the Mainstream: The Selected Works of George Gerbner.* New York: Peter Lang.

Ofqual (2023) What Qualification Levels Mean. [online] Available at: www.gov.uk/what-different-qualification-levels-mean/list-of-qualification-levels (accessed 11 February 2024).

Richard, D (2012) *The Richard Review of Apprenticeships.* London: School for Startups

Smith, R and Duckworth, V (2022) *Transformative Teaching and Learning in Further Education: Pedagogies of Hope and Social Justice.* Bristol: Policy Press

Windle, J (2010) 'Anyone Can Make It, but There Can Only Be One Winner': Modelling Neoliberal Learning and Work on Reality Television. *Critical Studies in Education*, 51(3): 251–3.

Wolf, A (2011) *The Review of Vocational Education: The Wolf Report.* London: DfE.

2 Learning

2.1 INTRODUCTION

This chapter starts by looking at what is meant by skills and knowledge (section 2.2). Different ways of learning are examined in section 2.3 under the following headings: apprenticeships, one-to-one training, blended learning, augmented and virtual realities, group learning, practice and reflective practice. Section 2.4 focuses on learning theories, with reference to neuroscience, behaviourism, constructivism and communities of practice. Motivation to learn is discussed in section 2.5, reflecting on how this links to deep, surface and strategic learning, as well as to the importance of mindset.

Task

- Think of a skill you learned. It does not have to be work related. It could, for example, be swimming, juggling, riding a bicycle, playing a musical instrument or learning another language.
- How did you learn?
- What enabled you to improve or maintain that skill?
- Are you still as good? If yes, why? If no, why?
- Make a list of the factors that helped you to learn this skill, and we will come back to this at the end of the chapter.
- If you're studying with colleagues, discuss your thoughts with each other.

2.2 SKILLS AND KNOWLEDGE

This book focuses on learning and teaching *skills*. This is not to suggest that *knowledge* is unimportant. While skills are practical and knowledge is theoretical, the two are inextricably linked.

TV shows reflect a division between knowledge and skills. Popular programmes such as *Mastermind*, *University Challenge*, *The Chase* and *Who Wants to Be a Millionaire?* celebrate participants' recall of facts, many of which may seem obscure to viewers.

Other programmes like *The Great British Bake Off*, *Strictly Come Dancing*, *MasterChef*, *Dancing on Ice*, *The Great British Sewing Bee* and *The Great Pottery Throw Down* focus on the contestants' ability to *do* rather than to *know*. In these shows, viewers watch the participants as they go on a 'journey' of practice, success and sometimes failure in demonstrating the skills they learn.

With the knowledge-rich TV programmes, viewers do not know how or why contestants have acquired their knowledge. It is evident, though, that they have developed a range of skills to learn facts and to recall them quickly when necessary. Participants in the skills-based shows come to competitions with existing knowledge. For example, on the cooking and baking shows, participants are not necessarily at the same starting point, but they can identify and explain various ingredients, techniques and tools. They make progress at a different pace, and they all deepen their knowledge as they develop their technical skills.

Task

- Thinking about the skill you identified in the first task in this chapter, what knowledge informed the development of that skill? For example, did you learn to read music to play an instrument?

Learning skills in the further education sector

As outlined in Chapter 1, the FE sector is remarkably diverse. The vast range of courses on offer are described using terms such as vocational, technical, academic, professional, recreational or applied. Implicit in the label is an indication of the balance between knowledge and skills. Academic courses are generally considered to be knowledge rich, while other programmes are more practical and job focused.

Describing FE as the *skills* sector risks reinforcing an age-old academic versus vocational divide, with the assertion that abstract knowledge is worthier than practical skills. Duckworth and Smith (2018) note that successive governments have seen FE as a route for vocational courses suited to young people who are not academic. Playfair (2019) outlines the problems of pitting skills against knowledge and argues that students need both, regardless of what they are studying. He suggests that what makes knowledge useful is '*the connecting and reconnecting of the things we know to each other, and the fluency with which we can mobilise those mental schemas of linked knowledge that help us understand, recall and apply*'.

When devising a plan for the term or year, teachers determine what knowledge and skills students need to learn and when. Recognising what students cannot yet do or understand at a particular stage is what Vygotsky (1978) described as the 'zone of proximal development' (ZPD). The ZPD occurs when existing knowledge and/or skills are insufficient for individuals or the group to be able to move on. The teacher needs to scaffold a phased introduction to progressively more difficult concepts or activities, in order for students to progress beyond their current level. Students may be held back, for example, if they struggle to master threshold concepts or skills.

Threshold concepts

A threshold concept refers to a concept that, when grasped by students, transforms the way they understand a whole subject. It allows them to move on in their learning. Threshold concepts are described as transformative (so that students have a significant shift in understanding); usually irreversible (difficult to unlearn); integrative (they reveal the big picture to the student); and often troublesome (difficult to grasp, counter-intuitive) (Meyer and Land, 2003).

Examples of the most basic threshold concepts in mathematics are addition, subtraction, multiplication and division. Mastering these operations is essential for working with other mathematics concepts, such as ratios, fractions and percentages.

When asked in an interview by National Numeracy, a charity that promotes everyday numeracy skills, why mathematics is important to baking, a *Great British Bake Off* finalist, Ian Cumming, responded:

> *There is more maths involved in baking than you might expect. When you look at some of the things which went wrong for me, you could definitely put that down to a lapse in maths. At one stage I had to use Pi in the final showstopper to calculate the area of the cakes.*
>
> (National Numeracy, 2015)

Mathematical errors can be critical, even life-threatening, in the real world of kitchens, salons, factories, laboratories and construction sites. On TV programmes, they are not as perilous, but a miscalculation can make a difference in terms of winners and evictions. For example, mathematics played a key role in an episode of *The Great British Sewing Bee*. Judges were looking for precision and regular squares in one episode when contestants had 3 hours and 45 minutes to make a kilt. Not all contestants demonstrated the same mathematical skill level as they digested the instructions about the size of the tartan repeat. Starting with 1.5 metres of fabric, contestants had to calculate how to evenly pleat the kilt and how much to reduce each pleat by to form a waist. In an episode of *MasterChef*, a contestant miscalculated the amount of baking soda for her chocolate cake. As a result, the cake was dense and unappetising, and she was eliminated from the competition.

Threshold skills

Mastering basic knife skills is one of the most essential parts of learning to cook. Many types of knives are used in professional kitchens and most have the potential to be dangerous if not used correctly. As well as helping to develop quicker and more effective knife skills, proper training minimises the risk of injury. In welding, sewing, hairdressing or beauty therapy, hand–eye co-ordination and attention to detail are critical skills that need to be honed. In dance or ice skating, balance involves having a strong core and being able to distribute weight evenly between both feet. Students cannot move on to more advanced dance or skating moves until they have mastered this skill.

Task

- In the subject you teach, pick a particular skill your students need to learn. What *knowledge* is linked to that skill? For example, when learning about basic knife skills, students also need to know about health and safety requirements.
- What are the threshold concepts and skills in your subject?
- To what extent is mathematics integral to the subject(s) you teach?

2.3 WAYS OF LEARNING

In this section, we look at the various ways in which people learn skills.

Task

- Imagine you are asked to grout tiles in a bathroom. Assuming you do not already possess this skill, would you:
  - find and watch a YouTube clip explaining how to grout tiles?
  - read the relevant section of a book?
  - try to find a short course you could enrol on?
  - ask a friend/relative to show you?
  - go to a hardware shop and ask for the relevant materials, read the instructions on the packaging and then have a go?
- What determined your choice? Is your choice about how you think you learn best or simply convenience?
- Ask friends, colleagues and relatives the same question. What conclusions do you draw from their responses?

Observation

Many of those undertaking this task will have chosen the first option. The use of technology to observe people modelling desirable actions and behaviour has been an instructional technique for a long time. For example, Arkenback (2023) notes that after World War II, corporations made human relations training films. She suggests that these were to shape managers' and workers' thinking within and beyond the workplace. Also, the Open University, founded in 1969, broadcast TV instructional programmes at specific times, in addition to supplying its students with printed materials.

Ofcom's Media Nations Report (2022), investigating the type of short-form videos people watch, found 'how to' content, such as recipes or DIY, are the most viewed. The rapid expansion of online video production and viewing is in part due to the fact that learning content is being designed by ordinary people and not necessarily formally authored by publishers or educational institutions.

Callan and Johnston's (2020) study of social media adoption in Australian vocational education and training institutions notes that YouTube videos align with their aim to have more self-paced learning. Indeed, some trade teachers reported that their apprentices preferred YouTube as a way to learn hands-on practical skills.

Reasons for self-learning, with or without technology, vary. For some it is about convenience, particularly as the internet, smart phones and apps continue to provide the flexibility and freedom to learn whenever and wherever you wish. For others it may be about cost, feeling in control, or the fact that this type of learning is free from the stress of assessment and examinations associated with more formal methods of learning. Seemingly, numerous Nobel Prize winners, writers, musicians, scientists, actors, engineers and inventors claim to be autodidacts, that is, partially or wholly self-taught.

Learning from observation is a feature of many of the skills-based TV programmes. Contestants observe and then replicate what an expert creates. For example, in *The Great Pottery Throw Down*, participants watch a master potter wheel throwing and then attempt to create the same type of clay object. Similarly, established chefs demonstrate dishes on *MasterChef* that contestants then need to produce.

Apprenticeships

The idea of learning from a 'master' has been around for centuries. In Europe, the medieval guild system played a significant role in the development and regulation of apprenticeships from the twelfth century onwards.

The features of an apprenticeship varied depending on the time period and the trade or craft in question. An apprentice, often as young as 14 or 15, would live with the master and learn the skills and techniques necessary to become a skilled crafts or tradesperson. At the end of the apprenticeship, the apprentice would produce a masterpiece, and this would be assessed by a panel of experts, who would determine whether the apprentice had successfully completed their training and could work independently.

Although the image of an apprenticeship brings to mind a master mentoring a young trainee, studies reveal a more complex set of social relationships through which learning takes place and the term 'community of practice', to be explored later in this chapter, was coined to refer to the community that acts as a living curriculum for the apprentice (Lave and Wenger, 1991). Today, apprenticeships are still an important way for people to learn a trade or craft, up to and beyond graduate level across a range of professions. They have continued to evolve over time, with changes in technology, the economy and society influencing their development. Most often they combine on-the-job training and classroom instruction.

One-to-one training

Working intensely one to one with an expert is a feature of *Strictly Come Dancing*. Celebrities are allocated an experienced dancer to teach them to dance. These teachers, most of whom have represented their countries as professional dancers in international competitions, delight in sharing their passion and enthusiasm for dance. The celebrity may not live with the 'master', but they are with them every day, all day, for as long as they remain in the competition. They also draw on the extensive expertise of the wider 'Strictly community'. Each week contestants are judged by a panel of experts and viewers watching from home. Those who make it to the final weeks demonstrate considerable progress, reflecting the benefit of being taught by an expert, the intensity of the training and the many hours of practice.

Blended learning

Blended learning combines online activities and face-to-face teaching. This may include opportunities to interact with other students either asynchronously (accessing materials at different times) or synchronously (in real time, with students and the teacher attending together from different locations).

During the Covid-19 pandemic (2020–2022) blended learning became the norm, out of necessity, for students in all education sectors. This was particularly challenging in FE for the development of practical, technical skills.

Augmented and virtual realities

Post-pandemic, some blended learning remains out of choice, but skills-based practical training is primarily face to face in FE. However, augmented reality (AR) and virtual reality (VR) technologies are increasingly making it possible for students to explore a wide range of practical, technical skills in depth that they might otherwise not experience.

AR and VR create highly engaging educational experiences. For example, engineering trainees can learn to repair equipment or vehicles safely and properly in VR simulations. Construction trainees can perform complex electrical maintenance or feel what is like to stand on the scaffolding of a high rise building for the first time. Those training to be tree surgeons can experience climbing a tree with a safety harness and helmet, without endangering themselves or colleagues.

Group learning

Most learning in FE takes place with a teacher and a group of students in classrooms, workplaces, laboratories, training kitchens, salons or construction workshops.

In these settings, students will spend some of their time working together in pairs or small groups. The pros and cons vary depending on the context and the activity. At its best, group working for students leads to increased motivation, more effective communication and enhanced problem-solving skills. It can also improve students' subject knowledge and skills, as they can learn very effectively from each other. If a task involves taking on different roles within the group, students may also learn leadership and team-working skills.

While the team-based programmes *University Challenge* and *Only Connect* might reflect some of these advantages, most of the reality TV programmes are competitions with just one individual winner and often a significant prize. This leads to a strange dynamic whereby participants seemingly work together but, in effect, do all they can to outwit their colleagues and promote themselves.

For example, in the 'pressure test' in *MasterChef*, contestants work a shift at a busy restaurant under the supervision of a professional chef. In this setting, contestants need to demonstrate good team-working skills, as this is essential in a restaurant kitchen, but they know they are in competition with other participants.

The conflict between outshining others and, at the same time, demonstrating good teamwork is perhaps most stark in *The Apprentice*. In this programme, candidates are competing for a significant investment in their business from a successful businessperson. They are divided into two teams and given a series of business-themed tasks. The two nominated project leaders are meant to demonstrate good leadership, while the others display their team-working skills. Any loyalty to the team shown during the task is hastily abandoned once the losing team are left to reflect on why they failed to win and who among them should be fired. At this point, candidates engage in clichéd backbiting.

Task

- From what you know of *The Apprentice*, which of the statements in Table 2.1 do you agree with and why?

Table 2.1 Task with statements about *The Apprentice*

The Apprentice ...	
• is entertaining and engaging	• is too competitive and cut-throat
• provides contestants with a high level of exposure and publicity and can boost their careers	• is focused on drama and entertainment and gives an unrealistic portrayal of business
• gives contestants the opportunity to learn from successful businesspeople	• lacks diversity and perpetuates stereotypes about who works in business
• is informative in highlighting the challenges of running a business	• promotes questionable values such as greed, arrogance and dishonesty

- What values do you want your students to learn from your teaching? Are you promoting certain values either implicitly or explicitly? If so, which ones?
- To what extent do you think it is your role as a teacher to promote diversity, through your use of language and teaching resources, and to challenge negative stereotypes through your teaching?

Garden Rescue incorporates some competition but is much gentler in its approach than *The Apprentice* and many other reality TV programmes. Two designers pitch their ideas to homeowners, who choose which one they prefer. The designer who loses then works with the successful designer to create the makeover. In effect, it does not matter who wins as the outcome is always a significantly improved garden for a deserving homeowner, informed by the knowledge and skills of experienced gardeners.

Task

- Create an activity for your students that has an element of competition but requires them to work together in teams.
- Include team-related skills in the learning outcomes, such as '*demonstrate ability to collaborate*' or '*demonstrate effective communication skills*'.

Practice makes perfect

Whether learning is face to face, virtual, blended, with a personal trainer, in a group or independent, practice is crucial when mastering a skill. Practice helps to improve and refine the abilities necessary to perform that skill effectively. With many skills, such as driving a car, sustaining a yoga posture or playing a musical instrument, consistent practice helps to develop muscle memory and mental processes, enabling people to perform the skill without conscious effort. In doing so, this can lead to improved performance, increased confidence, less anxiety and a greater sense of accomplishment.

In his best seller *Outliers* (2008), Gladwell argues that it takes 10,000 hours of intensive practice to master complex skills. He suggests that once you have gained the basics, what distinguishes one person from another is how hard they work at it. This has been disputed and others maintain that factors such as quality of tuition and perhaps even natural talent are just as significant. Ericsson et al (1993), in their research into learning to play a violin, suggest that extensive practice must be 'deliberate' to be effective and by this they mean under the guidance of a teacher. Celebrities on *Strictly Come Dancing* and *Dancing on Ice* quickly see the link between 'deliberate practice', success and their own sustained effort.

Regularly watching clips of themselves in earlier sessions confirms how much progress the celebrities in *Strictly Come Dancing* are making and motivates them to continue. In FE, teachers support students to succeed in their end qualification, but on the way they also know the value of helping students to recognise each small step. As explored in Chapter 4, this kind of ipsative assessment is not linked to comparison with others or meeting external criteria; it focuses on an individual's own progress since their previous performance.

Reflective practice

As is the norm for the reality TV entertainment genre, celebrities are required to share emotions and confessions to camera. Of course, this is not a practice found in education.

Although this confessional approach may seem false, and even uncomfortable for educators, the fact that participants discuss their progress with the professional coaches and reflect on advice and feedback does align with sound pedagogical practice. The celebrities are encouraged to identify their strengths and to articulate exactly what they need to do next, not just to remain in the competition but to challenge themselves and further develop their skills.

This type of reflection echoes Kolb's experiential learning cycle (1984), as shown in Figure 2.1, that divides the learning process into four components: concrete experience (the weekly dance); reflective observation (discussion with coach and self-reflection, taking on board judges' feedback); abstract conceptualisation (identifying areas for improvement); and active experimentation (the next weekly dance).

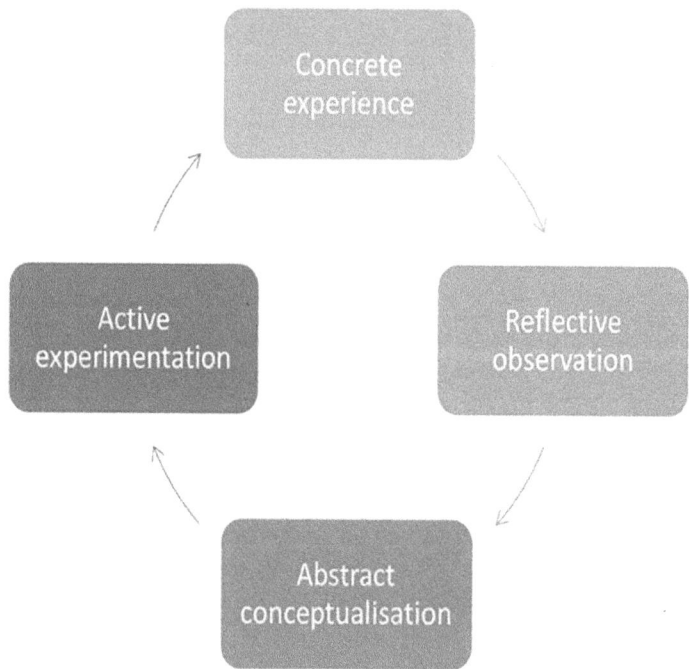

Figure 2.1 Kolb's experiential learning cycle

Kolb's experiential learning cycle is used extensively to inform professional practice across all sectors, as are various adaptations and other models. For example, Driscoll (2007) developed a framework for reflection for healthcare professionals with just three questions: *What? So What? Now What?* Whichever model you use, it is likely that, as well as encouraging your students to reflect on their work and progress in this way, you will be doing the same in terms of reflecting on your own practice as a teacher, trainer or trainee.

2.4 LEARNING THEORIES

Do we each have our own unique learning style? Bates (2019, p 117) describes a learning style as '*an idiosyncratic way in which an individual acquires, processes, comprehends and retains information*'. It is assumed people have their own preference as to how they learn, and this can be a dominant feature in all situations or, most likely, it will vary according to the context.

The concept of learning styles has been widely discussed and debated among educational researchers and practitioners. Most theories on learning styles require people to complete a questionnaire. For example, if you adopt the VARK model, you will find out if you are, in the main, a visual, auditory, reading or kinaesthetic learner (VARK Learning Styles, nd). With the Honey and Mumford model (1992) you could be identified as predominantly one of the following: an activist, a reflector, a theorist or a pragmatist.

Thorough research on the various learning styles models, undertaken by Coffield (2004), concluded that they are far too simplistic to be of any real value to either teachers or students, with no hard evidence that students' learning is enhanced by teaching tailored to their perceived learning style.

The literature on learning theories is extensive. Learning is a complex phenomenon and there is no universally accepted theory about how people learn. However, there is a broad consensus among educators that active engagement by students is important for meaningful learning. Active learning is usually taken to mean 'doing', reading, writing, discussing or problem-solving, rather than simply listening or observing. Clearly, developing a technical skill, such as cutting hair, welding, performing cardiopulmonary resuscitation (CPR) or plastering a wall requires the student to be active. A key challenge for teachers when teaching practical skills is to integrate the underpinning theoretical knowledge in a way that is active and engaging, and this will be explored in Chapter 3.

Harasim (2017) argues that learning theories are not just high-level abstractions. She suggests that an understanding of learning theories can inform teachers' professional practice. In fact, it is likely that teachers adopt their own educational theories, either consciously or subconsciously, and that this shapes how they teach and the assumptions they make about how their students learn (Harper, 2013; Harasim, 2017). Reviewing just a few of the many theories and approaches – neuroscience, behaviourism, constructivism and communities of practice – provides some insight into different perspectives on how people learn.

Neuroscience

Neuroscience is an evolving field of scholarship. It is the scientific study of the brain and nervous system. A key finding is that when people learn something new, there are physical changes that occur in the brain. This can involve the creation of new neural connections or the strengthening of existing ones. Repeated exposure to new information or skills can help strengthen the neural pathways involved in learning. This is why practice is necessary for the mastery of skills.

The brain does not simply passively absorb information. Neuroscience highlights the importance of emotions which can enhance or inhibit learning. Positive emotions, such as curiosity and excitement, can make learning more effective, while negative emotions, such as anxiety and stress, can hinder it. The fact the brain is constantly changing means we can continue to learn throughout our lives.

Behaviourism

Behaviourism is rooted in late nineteenth-century studies into how people behave. It is most widely associated with stimulus–response, reinforcement and repetition.

In explaining behaviourism, two experiments by Pavlov (1927) and Skinner (1958) are often cited. Pavlov famously conditioned a dog to associate food with the ringing of a bell. Initially the dog salivated when offered food. A bell ringing did not provoke a reaction from the dog. Food was then offered at the same time as the bell rang out, and this was repeated many times. Thereafter, when the bell rang, the dog salivated even if no food was offered.

In Skinner's well-known experiment, a rat in a box pressed a lever. The rat was rewarded with food and so associated the lever with food and repeated the process. When put on an electric grid and punished with an electric shock, the rat associated the grid with pain and so avoided the grid.

So, what does this have to do with teaching and learning? Behaviourists argue that like Pavlov's dog or Skinner's rat, students' behaviour can be learned and modified. Students will repeat behaviour when rewarded by the teacher, but not when they are punished.

Critics argue that behaviourism is outdated and based on unethical research. It does not engage with how the mind influences learning and why people who experience the same teaching do not all learn the same content equally. Despite its shortcomings, behaviourism has its merits, and it underpins much teaching and learning practice in FE, particularly in relation to repetition, reinforcement and feedback in the mastery of skills.

Task

- Read below summaries of two TV episodes: one from *Supernanny* and one from *The Dog Academy*.
- Drawing on these summaries, list the pros and cons of behaviourism in learning.
- To what extent do you use behaviourist approaches in your teaching?

Case study

Supernanny

In *Supernanny* a professional nanny helps parents who are struggling with their children's behaviour. Through observation and instructions, she demonstrates different ways to discipline children.

In one episode (Series 7, Episode 6, Channel 4, 2013), a mother is frustrated by her daughter's behaviour. Every time the toddler cries, the mother picks her up, but this does not stop the crying. The nanny gives the mother clear instructions, which she follows meticulously. The nanny watches as the following scene unfolds. The child screams and puts her arms out and the mother tells her that she cannot hold her now as she is cooking dinner. The toddler continues to scream and then hits her mother. The mother tells her daughter that if she does that again she will go on the 'naughty chair' for timeout. The toddler continues to cry and lash out. The mother takes her daughter to the chair at the other end of the room and keeps taking her back to the chair every time she refuses to stay. When the toddler is a little calmer, the mother tells her that she can help her mother with the cooking if she says sorry for her behaviour earlier. She refuses initially but after several returns to the chair, the toddler apologises to her mother. Calm is restored.

Case study

The Dog Academy

In *The Dog Academy* a team of specialist trainers educate frustrated owners in dog management skills and dog psychology. Dogs and their owners receive separate training designed to help owners build long-lasting, positive relationships with their dogs. Audiences are offered a chance to see how dogs and owners get on as they try to apply their new skills.

In one episode (Series 1, Episode 2, Channel 4, 2023), a couple have trouble with their dalmatian who, when they are outdoors, pulls excessively on the lead and drags them along, so much so that the dog has caused injury to its owners. The specialists explain that the dog has learned that a tight lead gives him access to an area ahead that he wants to explore and so he associates pulling hard with success. They train the dog, changing his behaviour, and then train the owners.

The key is for the person holding the lead to stand still when the dog pulls, rather than pull back. They then need to move slightly, wait for the dog to look back, give the dog a visual clue (thumbs up) and then an edible treat. The dog is rewarded for good behaviour and learns quickly that walks are only possible if he stays close on a loose lead. The owners each repeat the process several times until they get it right and are confident. The specialists emphasise the importance of both owners taking the same action, as lack of consistency will confuse the dog. They also assert that eventually the treat will not be necessary.

Constructivism

The constructivist approach suggests that people construct their own understanding and knowledge through their experiences, reflections and interactions with others. Learning is an active and iterative process of making meaning.

Understanding aspects of constructivism may explain why after a film in a cinema or a talk in a lecture theatre, however engaging, the individuals in the audience will leave with different interpretations. This is because they have each been influenced by their experience, values, beliefs and existing knowledge. Similarly, 12 people on a jury will not necessarily come to the same conclusion as to the innocence or guilt of the accused, even though they hear the same evidence from witnesses and the prosecution and defence lawyers (Harper, 2013).

Gogglebox documents families and groups of friends around the United Kingdom who are filmed while they observe and react to the previous week's television from their own homes.

Often *Gogglebox* households, and even individuals within a household group, react differently to what they see, even though they are watching the same programme. This reflects the fact that they each relate the new knowledge they gain from watching a programme to existing knowledge. For example, in one episode (Series 21, Episode 6), they watch an excerpt from a BBC dramatisation of *Great Expectations*. While they all find the segment when Pip meets Estella and Miss Havisham for the first time dark, disturbing and dramatic, their observations and comments vary considerably. This is because some are very familiar with the novel, two friends vaguely remember reading it at school, and two others had never heard of the book or of its author, Charles Dickens.

Task

- Think about a topic, concept or skill that you have taught or will teach.
- How can you accommodate students' differing levels of prior knowledge, skill and experience?

Communities of practice

Lave and Wenger (1991) suggest that socially situated learning takes place when people learn together collectively. They refer to this as 'communities of practice', as noted earlier in this chapter when discussing apprenticeships. Communities of practice are groups who share an interest, concern or a passion for something, and they learn by working together. The success of situated learning experiences relies on social interaction, and within an educational setting, students construct their own knowledge from the experiences they bring to the learning context. As a teacher, trainer or trainee, you may be part of a community engaged in peer-to-peer professional development activities.

Castaway 2000 came closer to a community of practice than other reality TV programmes. It followed a group of 36 men, women and children as they built, over a year, a sustainable self-sufficient society from scratch on a remote Scottish island. Unlike other TV reality programmes, there was no supporting film crew. The castaways filmed themselves, as it was thought that too many camera operators would undermine the sense of isolation. Also, as the aim was to build a community, there were no winners, no prizes and no evictions.

This format is now rare, possibly because it is the competition element in reality TV that makes watching at the time of broadcast more exciting, as with a sports event. People want to know who won or who was evicted. In doing so terrestrial channels maximise audience numbers, and this is particularly important to them at a time when they are under threat from other channels and streaming services.

Armitage et al (2016, p 72) suggest that an emphasis on developing an atmosphere of cooperation among students in FE can lead to a fear of creating a competitive spirit in the classroom. They argue that competitiveness is linked with achievement and doing one's best and they pose the following question: *'is it possible that the effect of discouraging competition is to damage motivation and ultimately the fulfilment of individual aspiration and potential?'*

Task

- What do you consider the pros and cons of using competition in teaching?
- Some FE providers give prizes to the students who have the best attendance and/or punctuality. What is your view on this practice, as a way of motivating students to attend and to be punctual?

2.5 MOTIVATION TO LEARN

Contestants who sign up for a reality TV programme have their own reasons to participate and are motivated to engage and to do their best. This is not necessarily always the case in FE. Understanding what motivates students to learn can help teachers to provide appropriate support.

Intrinsic or extrinsic?

Intrinsic motivation is driven by personal satisfaction and enjoyment rather than external rewards such as money or praise. People who are intrinsically motivated engage in an activity because it is satisfying, interesting or fulfilling in some way. Those who are extrinsically motivated participate primarily to gain or avoid something.

Task

- Think back to the first task in this chapter when you were asked to think of a skill you learned.
- Try to remember what motivated you. Were you persuaded by friends or relatives? Were you offered a reward if successful?

In interviews and to-camera confessionals, participants in TV programmes tend to focus on their intrinsic motivation to participate. They highlight how they have always wanted to learn how to garden, cook, bake, sew, ice skate or re-decorate their homes. In the case of *Freeze the Fear with Wim Hof*, where celebrities face a set of challenges in sub-zero temperatures, they explain that their motivation is about facing their own fears so that they can gain more control over their mind and body.

Nadiya Hussain, a winner of *The Great British Bake Off*, explained in interviews that she was motivated to challenge herself as a way of overcoming her panic disorder (Long, 2017). Bill Bailey, a *Strictly Come Dancing* winner, suggested in conversation in a podcast with Rob Brydon (2022) that being identified as the underdog and even a 'joke' participant early in the competition spurred him on to work even harder.

One might reasonably assume that, for many, the motivation to participate in a reality TV programme has an extrinsic element. People are attracted by financial rewards, lucrative employment opportunities, fame, titles and potential spin-off TV appearances and book deals. In some programmes, only the winner benefits. In others, all contestants are paid for their participation. Where there is no payment, there may still be elements of extrinsic motivation beyond simply receiving a trophy.

A more unusual, socially conscious and inclusive approach was taken in 2002 by chef Jamie Oliver in *Jamie's Kitchen*. In this series he attempted to train a group of 15 disadvantaged young people who, when they completed their course, were offered jobs in his not-for-profit restaurant Fifteen. Of the original cohort, 12 completed the programme, and at the time the show attracted approximately 5.4 million viewers. After 17 years and around 150 graduates, the restaurant closed but former trainees, who now work as chefs, were full of praise when interviewed (Iqbal, 2019). One said:

> *Being accepted as a Fifteen graduate on Jamie's Kitchen totally changed my life for the better, forever. Jamie ... chipped in when we couldn't pay rent and listened when we were finding it all a bit much. He took a chance on me when I was an unemployed 23-year-old and living in a hostel ... I felt stuck and was finding it really hard to get work. I was looking for something to believe in.*

In FE, there are no cash prizes. Students' extrinsic motivation is usually linked to the prospect of gaining a qualification, progressing to a higher level, or getting a job or promotion. Sometimes this extrinsic driver is sufficient for them to complete their programme.

Deep, surface and strategic learning

Although intrinsic motivation is more likely to lead to 'deep' learning, while extrinsic motivation is associated with 'surface' learning, research suggests that these are not stable traits in an individual (Marton and Säljö, 1976). In effect, people may use both approaches at different times, even if they have an overall preference for one or the other.

Students who adopt a surface approach tend to focus on regurgitating facts or reproducing material for assessments, without the desire to understand what they have been taught. They often cut corners to get tasks out of the way, and they are more likely to be cynical about the activities teachers ask them to undertake. In contrast, those who take a deep approach are motivated by interest rather than simply by assessment requirements. They are more likely to link new ideas to their previous knowledge.

What is known as 'strategic learning' subtly combines both deep and surface learning strategies depending on the task at hand. Strategic learners know when, where and how to take a surface approach while keeping an eye on the big picture and on high-level outcomes.

Mindset

In FE, as discussed earlier, students on technical programmes need to understand and use mathematics, whether it is to measure and scale ingredients or to build, install and repair houses, products or vehicles, or to create and send invoices. Even if they enjoy their main programme of study, many students have a negative mindset towards mathematics, especially if they are required to re-sit a GCSE. There may be many reasons for this negative mindset. The idea that the subject is inherently difficult, or that some people are simply destined not to be good at it, is pervasive. Poor experience of mathematics at school, repeated failure and adults who think it is socially acceptable to laugh off how they 'hate maths' can all reinforce this mindset.

Expectancy theory asserts that to be motivated, people must have both the *desire* for the outcome and the *expectancy* that they can obtain that goal (Vroom, 1964). With this in mind, even those students who place a high value on understanding mathematics and gaining the qualification will not be motivated if they are convinced they will fail.

Since the early 2000s, there has been growing interest in education sectors in the links between motivation, learning and students' self-belief. Dweck (2006) suggests that some people have a 'fixed' mindset and see ability as innate and fixed from birth and so think you cannot do much to change it. Others have a 'growth' mindset and believe you can *develop your skills and talents through hard work, the right strategies and guidance from others*.

The two mindsets lead to very different responses to learning situations, as reflected in Table 2.2. Those with a fixed mindset are likely to look for reassurance by doing things they are comfortable with. If they have a growth mindset, they are likely to acknowledge hard work and strive to improve when they have underachieved. Also, they look for challenges, particularly when there is an opportunity to learn something new.

Table 2.2 Mindsets

Situation	A fixed mindset	✓	A growth mindset	✓
At the start of a task or course	I hope it is easy.		I hope it is interesting.	
When it begins to get difficult	This is too hard.		This may take some time to grasp.	
You get poor feedback from a teacher	This proves I'm no good.		I need to take the feedback on board and do better next time.	
You are given a difficult task	This will show how useless I am.		This is a chance to challenge myself.	
You make a mistake	I give up.		I'll try again, using a different approach.	
You do very well on an assignment	Great. I'm a natural.		Great. My hard work paid off.	

(adapted from FutureLearn, University of Groningen, nd)

Task

- Reflecting on your own mindset, for each situation in Table 2.2 tick which thought is closer to your approach to learning.
- To what extent do you recognise these two mindsets in your students?

2.6 CONCLUSION

People learn in different ways. How you learned when you were younger, how you approach a challenge, how much effort you put in and how motivated you are will all play a part. Revisit the list you made for the first task in this chapter of the factors that helped you to learn a skill. Some of these factors may relate to what someone, possibly a teacher, did to help you. Teachers may have no control over the external factors that influence their students, but *what* and *how* they teach can have a significant impact on students' learning. This is explored in the next chapter.

REFERENCES

Arkenback, C (2023) YouTube as a Site for Vocational Learning: Instructional Video Types for Interactive Service Work in Retail. *Journal of Vocational Education & Training*. https://doi.org/10.1080/13636820.2023.2180423

Armitage, A, Cogger, A, Evershed, J, Hayes, D, Lawes, S and Renwick, M (2016) *Teaching in Post-14 Education and Training*. 5th ed. Maidenhead: McGraw-Hill Education/Open University Press.

Bates, B (2019) *Learning Theories Simplified*. 2nd ed. London: Sage.

Brydon, R (2022) Bill Bailey's Incredible Experience of Winning Strictly Come Dancing. [online] Available at: www.youtube.com/watch?v=nfGFkBnsXu4 (accessed 11 February 2024).

Callan, V J and Johnston, M A (2020) Influences Upon Social Media Adoption and Changes to Training Delivery in Vocational Education Institutions. *Journal of Vocational Education & Training*, 74(4): 1–26.

Channel 4 (2013) *Supernanny*. [online] Available at: www.youtube.com/watch?v=6S04J3QLHdE (accessed 16 May 2023).

Channel 4 (2023) *The Dog Academy*, Episode 2, 6 April 2023. [online] Available at: https://www.channel4.com/programmes/the-dog-academy/on-demand/73756-002 (accessed 11 February 2024).

Coffield, F, Moseley, D, Hall E and Ecclestone, K (2004) *Learning Styles and Pedagogy in Post-16 Learning: A Systematic and Critical Review*. London: Learning and Skills Research Centre, Learning and Skills Development Agency.

Driscoll, J (ed) (2007) *Practising Clinical Supervision: A Reflective Approach for Healthcare Professionals*. Edinburgh: Balliere Tindall.

Duckworth, V and Smith, R (2018) Breaking the Triple Lock: Further Education and Transformative Teaching and Learning. *Education & Training*, 60(6): 529–43.

Dweck, C S (2006) *Mindset: The New Psychology of Success*. Random House.

Ericsson, K A, Krampe, R T and Tesch-Römer, C (1993) The Role of Deliberate Practice in the Acquisition of Expert Performance. *Psychological Review*, 100(3): 363–406.

FutureLearn, University of Groningen (nd) Fixed and Growth Mindset. [online] Available at: www.futurelearn.com/info/courses/improving-study-techniques/0/steps/55541 (accessed 11 February 2024).

Gladwell, M (2008) *Outliers*. Back Bay Books.

Harasim, L (2017) *Learning Theory and Online Technologies*. 2nd ed. New York; Abingdon: Routledge.

Harper, H (2013) *Outstanding Teaching in Lifelong Learning*. Milton Keynes: Open University Press.

Honey, P and Mumford, A (1992) *The Manual of Learning Styles*. Maidenhead: Peter Honey Publications.

Iqbal, N (2019) Jamie Oliver Gave Us Our Big Break in the Kitchen – and He's Still Our Hero. *The Guardian*, 26 May. [online] Available at: www.theguardian.com/food/2019/may/26/jamie-oliver-fifteen-gave-us-big-break-still-our-hero (accessed 11 February 2024).

Kolb, D (1984) *Experiential Learning: Experience as the Source of Learning and Development*. Prentice Hall.

Lave, J and Wenger, E (1991) *Situated Learning: Legitimate Peripheral Participation*. Cambridge: Cambridge University Press.

Long, N (2017) Friday Talks to Bake-off Queen Nadiya Hussain. Gulf News, 24 March. [online] Available at: https://gulfnews.com/friday/art-people/friday-talks-to-bake-off-queen-nadiya-hussain-1.1997115 (accessed 11 February 2024).

Marton, F and Säljö, R (1976) On Qualitative Differences in Learning: Outcome and Process. *British Journal of Educational Psychology*, 46: 4–11.

Meyer, J and Land, R (2003) *Threshold Concepts and Troublesome Knowledge: Linkages to Ways of Thinking and Practising within the Disciplines Project*. [online] Available at: www.etl.tla.ed.ac.uk/docs/ETLreport4.pdf (accessed 11 February 2024).

National Numeracy (2015) Great British Bake Off Finalist Champions the Importance of Everyday Maths. [online] Available at: www.nationalnumeracy.org.uk/news/great-british-bake-finalist-champions-importance-everyday-maths (accessed 11 February 2024).

Ofcom (2022) *Media Nations 2022*. [online] Available at: www.ofcom.org.uk/research-and-data/tv-radio-and-on-demand/media-nations-reports/media-nations-2022 (accessed 11 February 2024).

Pavlov, I P (1927) *Conditioned Reflexes: An Investigation of the Physiological Activity of the Vertebrate Cortex*. London: Oxford University Press.

Playfair, E (2019) Why Pit Knowledge Against Skills? *Times Educational Supplement*, 19 April. [online] Available at: https://www.tes.com/magazine/archived/why-knowledge-vs-skills-false-dichotomy (accessed 11 February 2024).

Skinner, B F (1958) Reinforcement Today. *American Psychologist*, 13: 94–9.

VARK Learning Styles (nd) VARK Modalities: What do Visual, Aural, Read/Write & Kinesthetic Really Mean? [online] Available at: https://vark-learn.com/introduction-to-vark/the-vark-modalities (accessed 11 February 2024).

Vroom, V (1964) *Work and Motivation*. New York: Wiley and Sons.

Vygotsky, L (1978) *Mind in Society: The Development of Higher Psychological Processes*. Cambridge, MA: Harvard University Press.

3 Teaching

3.1 INTRODUCTION

This chapter starts with an examination of what is meant by professionalism, with headings in section 3.2 on dual professionals and the Professional Standards. Next, the role of the FE teacher is discussed in section 3.3. Following this, section 3.4 examines pedagogy, with reference to generic, vocational, subject-specific and critical pedagogies. Planning teaching in section 3.5 explores teaching methods, assessment for learning, developing students' skills, one-to-one teaching and tutorials. The integration of theory into practical sessions, along with English and mathematics, is investigated in section 3.6. Technology is the subject of section 3.7, looking at its impact on the curriculum, as well as digital tools to support teaching and learning.

3.2 PROFESSIONALISM

What do these four people have in common?

1. Jayne Torvill who, with Christopher Dean, won a gold medal at the Winter Olympics in 1984. Their performance to the music of Ravel's *Boléro* was watched by a British television audience of 24 million people.
2. Motsi Mabuse, who won the South African Latin American dance championship eight times. She studied civil engineering at university before embarking on a career in ballroom dancing.
3. Charlie Dimmock, a gardening expert. She trained as an amenity horticulturalist and, having gained a distinction in a BTEC diploma, went on to further study while spending a year of her training at the Chelsea Physic Garden in London.
4. Monica Galetti, who worked as first commis chef at La Gavroche, a two-Michelin-starred restaurant, and then progressed to senior sous-chef. She also launched, and was Head Chef of, Le Gavroche des Tropiques in Mauritius.

These four women are presenters and/or judges on TV programmes. Their qualification to appear on television stems from their professional backgrounds. They are trusted and respected by viewers because they have been successful practitioners in their respective professions: ice skating, dance, gardening and cooking. When they make suggestions or give feedback to others, they know what they are talking about.

Dual professionals

This is not dissimilar to teaching in FE. As a student on a skills-based course, you may not be taught by world champions, but you expect teachers to have worked in the job you are training for, so that you can learn and benefit from their experience and expertise. However, having this occupational expertise is not enough. You also want them to be good teachers.

Professionalism is about demonstrating the knowledge, skills and behaviours expected of a person who is trained for a particular job. As reflected in the quotation below, FE teachers are expected to be professionals in not just one but *two* jobs.

> *The best vocational teaching and learning is a sophisticated process; it demands 'dual professionals' – teachers and trainers with occupational expertise and experience, who can combine this with excellent teaching and learning practice.*
> (Commission on Adult Vocational Teaching and Learning, 2013, p 7)

Professional standards

Professionalism is often articulated in a code of conduct or set of standards that reflect accepted practice within a particular occupation or profession. Specifically designed for FE, the *Professional Standards for Teachers and Trainers* were introduced in 2014 and updated in 2022 (see Figure 3.1).

The standards are intended to set out clear expectations of effective practice in education and training; enable teachers, trainers and trainees to identify areas for their own professional development; and provide a national reference point that organisations can use to support the development of their staff (Education and Training Foundation, 2022).

Take a look at the task below and see what your expectations of professional standards are.

Task

- Gordon Ramsay, the chef, swears and yells at those working in kitchens, supposedly to ensure and maintain high standards. If possible, watch a video clip of Gordon Ramsay in action on YouTube.
- Do you think his behaviour is 'professional'?
- If so, should teachers allow trainee chefs to behave in this way while training?
- If not, how do you justify his success to trainee chefs who want to emulate Gordon Ramsay's style?
- If you think a teacher allowing students to behave like Gordon Ramsay is unprofessional, which professional standard(s) do you think are relevant?

Professional Standards
for Teachers and Trainers in the Further Education and Training Sector

Professional Values and Attributes

Develop your own judgment of what works and does not work in your teaching and training.

1. Critically reflect on and evaluate your practices, values, and beliefs to improve learner outcomes.
2. Promote and embed education for sustainable development (ESD) across learning and working practices.
3. Inspire, motivate, and raise aspirations of learners by communicating high expectations and a passion for learning.
4. Support and develop learners' confidence, autonomy and thinking skills, taking account of their needs and starting points.
5. Value and champion diversity, equality of opportunity, inclusion and social equity.
6. Develop collaborative and respectful relationships with learners, colleagues and external stakeholders.
7. Engage with and promote a culture of continuous learning and quality improvement.

Professional Knowledge and Understanding

Develop deep and critically informed knowledge and understanding in theory and practice.

8. Develop and update knowledge of your subject specialism, taking account of new practices, research and/or industry requirements.
9. Critically review and apply your knowledge of educational research, pedagogy, and assessment to develop evidence-informed practice.
10. Share and update knowledge of effective practice with colleagues, networks and/or research communities to support improvement.
11. Develop and apply your knowledge of special educational needs and disabilities to create inclusive learning experiences.
12. Understand your teaching role and responsibilities and how these are influenced by legal, regulatory, institutional and ethical contexts.

Professional Skills

Develop your expertise and skills to ensure the best outcomes for learners.

13. Promote and support positive learner behaviour, attitudes and wellbeing.
14. Apply motivational, coaching and skill development strategies to help learners progress and achieve.
15. Plan and deliver learning programmes that are safe, inclusive, stretching and relevant to learners' needs.
16. Select and use digital technologies safely and effectively to promote learning.
17. Develop learners' mathematics, English, digital and wider employability skills.
18. Provide access to up-to-date information, advice and guidance so that learners can take ownership of their learning and make informed progression choices.
19. Apply appropriate and fair methods of assessment and provide constructive and timely feedback to support learning and achievement.
20. Develop enrichment and progression opportunities for learners through collaboration with employers, higher education and/or community groups.

Figure 3.1 The *Professional Standards for Teachers and Trainers*
Source: Education and Training Foundation, 2022

3.3 THE ROLE OF THE TEACHER

What is your role as a teacher? What sort of teacher do you want to be?

In the programme *Big Dreams, Small Spaces*, Monty Don, a well-known horticulturist, helps gardening enthusiasts to fulfil a gardening project they plan to undertake. He visits them, listens to their plans, gives advice, and then rolls up his sleeves and helps with the actual gardening. He leaves them for several months to get on with the project and then returns to answer their questions and concerns, review progress and provide practical support again if necessary. On his third and final visit, he observes – usually with admiration – what has been achieved and the enthusiasts reflect on what they have learned through the process.

In this scenario, Monty fulfils the role of a teacher. His role is critical, but he is not the sort of teacher who tells students what to do. He provides guidance, support and expertise but leaves his students (in this case volunteer gardening enthusiasts) to do the overwhelming majority of the work. They own the project: they research, design, source, chop, cut back, dig and plant. To inform what they plant, they investigate and consider a whole range of factors, such as soil type, sun location and plant hardiness. Most significantly, they learn by doing and researching. This reflects the type of active and deep learning discussed in the previous chapter.

In contrast, in *Ground Force*, a team of gardeners make over the garden of an individual who has been nominated by someone else. While the individual is away, the team gets friends and family to help them to make over the garden in a few days. This is an entertaining and successful TV programme, as it is always a well-deserved and wonderful surprise for the individual concerned. However, as a teaching model, it would be poor. In effect, the 'teachers' do all the work for the benefit of the 'student'. Although the outcome is excellent and all parties concerned are happy, the student does not engage at all in the process and so learns very little, if anything. This would be like a teacher making a product for their students that they then present as their own.

These are two extremes, and your own approach may be somewhere in the middle. You may wish to be more Monty and less *Ground Force*, but much will depend on the subject, the level and the context. Also, your approach may change over time as you gain experience and reflect on your own practice. It may well be that you pass through the three stages outlined by Biggs (1999, pp 21–4). First, you focus on the content you need to cover and think about how to make it as clear as possible and believe that it is then up to the students to attend lessons and to undertake the work you give them. You then move on to the second stage whereby you acknowledge the need to motivate students and maintain their interest, and so you adjust your teaching approach. In the last stage, you start your planning by focusing not on content or what *you* need to do, but on what *your students* need to do.

3.4 PEDAGOGY

Generic pedagogy

The standards listed under the core principle 'Professional Skills' relate to pedagogy. Orr (2018) suggests that a broad definition of pedagogy is one that describes how teachers explain the decisions they make in relation to a particular curriculum or body of knowledge, and to a particular student or group of students. This means that if you plan to show your students a video clip or ask them to complete a task, you should be able to explain why you have made these decisions.

The 'why' will depend on the context and on your understanding of how students learn. One view, rarely expressed in the FE sector these days, is that teaching skills flow naturally from subject expertise. Taking this stance, the assumption is that, for example, a good plumber or bricklayer can by definition teach these skills to others without the need for any teacher training. This view may even be associated with a mistrust of anything related to pedagogy (Robson, 2006).

A more widespread view, reflected in the Professional Standards, is that not only should FE teachers undertake some form of teacher training, but they also need to keep up to date with developments both in pedagogy and in their subject/occupational area.

Initial teacher education (ITE) tends to focus on *generic* pedagogy that can be applied across all disciplines. For example, trainee teachers who are sociologists, hairdressers, engineers and sports coaches are in lessons together learning about teaching. Usually, in discussions and in written assignments, trainees are expected to relate this generic pedagogy to their own discipline and context. It is usual practice for subject-specific mentors to support trainees in the workplace, if at all possible. In addition, if resources permit, in certain parts of the programme, there are subject-specific groupings, such as science or humanities. Sometimes there is a group called vocational or technical, on the assumption that there is a 'vocational pedagogy'.

Vocational pedagogy

The following definition for vocational pedagogy is not dissimilar to that suggested above by Kevin Orr in that it focuses on the decisions teachers make about the approach they use with their students.

> When I use the term 'vocational pedagogy' I mean 'the science, art and craft of teaching and learning vocational education'. Or you could say more simply that vocational pedagogy is the sum total of the many decisions which vocational teachers take as they teach, adjusting their approaches to meet the needs of learners and to match the context in which they find themselves.
>
> (Lucas, 2014, p 2)

Subject-specific pedagogy

There is an argument that generic, or even vocational, pedagogy does not have sufficient depth and that FE teachers, like those who train to teach in secondary schools, should focus more on *subject-specific* pedagogy, a distinctive pedagogy associated with individual subjects or related groups of subjects. Debates about subject-specific pedagogy in FE are not new, but they are complex for many reasons, not least of all due to the diversity of the FE curriculum and the varied combinations of traditional disciplines it draws upon (Orr et al, 2019).

It is evident that teachers need to know how to teach in ways that students can learn. To do this they should be able to recognise what makes certain aspects of the curriculum easy or difficult. For example, they should know whether it is better to interweave certain topics, skills or concepts and return to each one regularly, or to study one very thoroughly before moving on to the next. This is sometimes referred to as pedagogical content knowledge (PCK), a concept developed by Shulman in the 1980s. In effect, PCK is what distinguishes teachers from non-teaching specialists, for example a plumbing teacher from a plumber. PCK is described as:

> ... *that special amalgam of content and pedagogy that is uniquely the province of teachers, their own special form of professional understanding ... It represents the blending of content and pedagogy into an understanding of how particular topics, problems or issues are organised, represented, and adapted to the diverse interests and abilities of learners, and presented for instruction.*
>
> (Shulman, 1987, p 8)

Task

- Think about your own training and/or continuing professional development (CPD). Do you prefer working with others who teach the same subject or being in a mixed-discipline group? What are the pros and cons of each option? What can you learn from each group?
- Is PCK a concept you recognise? How does this relate to threshold concepts, as discussed in the previous chapter?
- With reference to one particular unit or module you teach, is it more effective to interweave topics, skills or concepts or to get students to study one at a time? Explain the rationale for your choice.

Critical pedagogy

Critical pedagogy, usually associated with Paulo Freire (1921–97), asserts that teaching should challenge learners to examine power structures and patterns of inequality within the status quo. Friere argues that teaching is not about 'depositing', whereby students receive, file and store information, kindly gifted to them by an all-knowing teacher. He argues that this 'banking' model of education *'negates education and knowledge as processes of inquiry'* (2017, p 45) and so has a disempowering effect on students. The antidote is to develop students' critical thinking skills, with a pedagogy that encourages participation. In doing so, students are more likely to want to change society and make it fairer for all.

Task

- To what extent do you think FE teachers should prepare students to adapt to the working world as it currently is, or to what it *could* or *should* be, by encouraging them to question and challenge current practices?
- Discuss with colleagues, if possible.

3.5 PLANNING TEACHING

Learning outcomes

Teachers in FE may not be able to choose their students or the curriculum, but they do provide the environment in which their students learn. They have considerable flexibility when it comes to planning, selecting, applying or adapting the teaching and assessment methods they use.

It is helpful to start lesson planning by asking what it is that you want your students to be able to do, demonstrate or produce. For example, if the learning outcomes for a beauty studies lesson are that students will be able to: *'(a) prepare for a themed face painting'* and *'(b) carry out a themed face painting'*, you plan your teaching and assessment accordingly to ensure that *all* students can demonstrate that they have met these outcomes. If the outcomes, teaching and assessment methods all neatly match, students are more likely to be successful. This is known as *constructive alignment* (Biggs, 1999) and is discussed in the next chapter.

> **Case study**
>
> *Glow Up*
>
> *Glow Up: Britain's Next Make-Up Star* is a reality TV programme devised to find new make-up artists. The contestants take part in weekly challenges to progress through the competition, and they are judged by industry professionals and weekly guest stars. In one episode (Series 5, Episode 3) the eight make-up artists are tasked with a real industry assignment to create special effects make-up to turn actors into deceased plague victims for a TV programme called *Ghosts*. With access to cutting-edge prosthetics and techniques, the make-up artists are required to demonstrate technical precision and artistic flair. The Head of Hair and Make-up Design for *Ghosts* outlines the project brief. She instructs the participants to work in pairs.

Task

- Why do you think she made the decision to ask the make-up artists to work in pairs? What might be the benefits and challenges of pair work in this particular scenario?
- Think of a lesson when you worked in a pair or group or when you asked your students to work in pairs or small groups. What was the rationale for the decision(s)? Be specific about what did or did not work well and why.

Teaching methods

It is generally acknowledged that the most effective teaching methods for skills-based programmes are those that provide opportunities for students to 'learn by doing', as well as include feedback, reflection and theory.

A variety of approaches is important given that, as explored in the previous chapter, people learn in different ways. It is helpful when planning and structuring lessons to think about what your students will be doing while you are 'teaching', as reflected in Table 3.1. This will clearly indicate how active, or passive, your students are at different points in your lesson. When students are observing or listening it does not necessarily mean they are inactive, as ideally they are concentrating on what they see or hear. Teachers soon learn how long their students can maintain concentration before they need to switch activities.

Table 3.1 Teaching approaches

What is the teacher doing?	What are students doing?
Giving demonstration	Observing
Talking, giving lecture	Listening, taking notes
Questions to whole group	Responding, answering
Leading whole group discussion	Responding, answering, asking questions
Listening	Giving presentations
Giving instructions for task	Listening, taking notes, asking questions
Observing, walking around, listening, answering questions, giving feedback, assessing	Making, constructing, creating, thinking
	Drawing, sketching, designing, calculating
	In groups or pairs undertaking practical or written task(s)
	Individually undertaking practical or written task(s)
	Engaged in games or assessments – face to face or virtually
	Undertaking role plays
	Problem-solving
	Having conversations/debating
	Coaching/teaching each other
	Peer assessing
	Experimenting
	Researching
	Typing/writing notes, blog, reflections

Assessment for learning (AfL)

Assessment is the subject of the next chapter, but AfL is mentioned here as it cannot be disentangled from day-to-day teaching. AfL recognises that every teaching and learning task or activity offers assessment opportunities. It provides a means of continuously assessing knowledge and skills, informing teaching and providing feedback to students. Skilled teachers routinely use question and answer to check and monitor students' understanding throughout a lesson. As can be seen in Table 3.1, teachers often spend time walking around and observing their students at work. For example, a make-up teacher may point out a mismatch of colours between the neck and face to a student who is creating special effects on a model. This is valuable feedback for the student, who can work immediately on improvements.

Developing students' skills

As noted in the previous chapter, active engagement by students is important for meaningful learning, particularly when developing technical skills. This may involve the students working as a whole group or working in smaller groups, either in pairs or individually.

Independent learning

> ### Task
>
> - Use YouTube, or any other video sharing website, to teach yourself one of the following:
>   - how to peel an onion without crying;
>   - how to say hello in ten languages;
>   - how to make perfect boiled eggs;
>   - how to whistle with your fingers;
>   - how to juggle;
>   - how to make a paper aeroplane.
> - Now ask yourself the following: did you succeed in mastering the task? If yes, how easy was it? If no, why not?
> - Teach someone else the same skill but without using YouTube or any other media.
> - How successful was this other person in learning the skill? Compare with them the two methods of learning – with a teacher and without a teacher.

Whatever the outcome of this task, there is no suggestion that FE does not need teachers. However, when planning your teaching, it is useful to think about how much students can do by themselves during or between lessons.

Independent working is important for students, as it helps prepare them for life beyond their current studies. The ability to learn and adapt on your own is crucial in an ever-changing world, where knowledge and skills become outdated very quickly. It can also help students to develop other skills, such as critical thinking, time management and problem-solving. There is a temptation to assume that a lesson in which students are working independently is easy to teach in that all the students can be given something 'to get on with'. In fact, the teacher needs to lay the groundwork by preparing students and gradually withdrawing support.

Many skills-based lessons start with a demonstration by the teacher. This provides students with the opportunity to see what the finished product, be it a main dish, clay pot or tiled roof, should look like and how an expert undertakes the task. Students may then be given instructions as to how to complete the task(s) themselves. With an instrumental and pragmatic focus on skills development, teachers are conditioning students to behave like chefs, potters or tilers. The fact that they focus on observable behaviour reflects elements of behaviourism, as discussed in the previous chapter. To encourage students to become independent, and more confident and proficient, teachers can ask them to work out the instructions themselves or provide them with only limited information.

Case study

The Great British Bake Off

In each episode of *The Great British Bake Off* there are three challenges: the signature, the technical and the showstopper. For the first and third, bakers have had an opportunity to plan, prepare and practise. For the second, the bakers are all given the same recipe at the same time and not told in advance what it will be. This challenge requires enough technical knowledge and experience to produce a certain finished product when given limited – or even minimal – instructions. For example, an instruction may be 'bake' without giving the required length of time in the oven or the temperature. The finished products are judged anonymously and ranked from worst to best.

Task

- What are the pros and cons of adopting this approach to the technical challenge, whereby there is no demonstration by an expert and students are given only limited instructions?
- To what extent would this approach work in your own discipline?
- How do you help your students to develop independent working skills?

Collaborative learning

Students need to be able to work on their own, and they also need to collaborate with others. Wherever they work – in a salon, kitchen, office, leisure centre or on a building site – students will most likely need to work with colleagues. FE teachers can provide opportunities for students to work alongside others.

In the previous chapter, *The Apprentice* was cited to demonstrate the conflict between outshining others and demonstrating good teamwork. In effect, in *The Apprentice* candidates are competing with each other even when in the same team. In contrast to this model, the whole team 'wins' in *DIY SOS: The Big Build* as they work together very effectively to meet a shared goal. It is a programme in which an experienced team, supported by volunteers, undertakes major building work to the property of individuals or families who have had a change in circumstances. Led by a project manager, the team usually consists of plasterers, plumbers, electricians, scaffolders and decorators. Throughout the programme viewers see how they work together, demonstrating that they can:

- listen to other people's ideas sympathetically and critically;
- think creatively;
- problem-solve;
- recognise and use other people's knowledge and skills;
- reflect on their own strengths;
- give and receive peer feedback;
- manage time effectively;
- see projects through to a conclusion;
- cope with group dynamics and conflict.

A group project for students does not have to be as large or complex as in *DIY SOS: The Big Build*, but it can be a vehicle for students to develop these same skills. Groupwork is ideally suited to problem-based learning, whereby students learn by actively engaging in real-world and personally meaningful projects. This kind of problem-based learning is associated with constructivism, as discussed in the previous chapter, as it is an active learning process rather than passive absorption, and students tackle authentic and realistic problems.

For example, it is not uncommon for business studies students in FE to undertake a group task whereby each group comes up with an idea for a new business. Drawing on research and what they have learned in their course so far, they create a business plan and then pitch the idea to classmates and several 'dragon' investors, as in the TV programme *Dragons' Den*. To promote sustainability, teachers may ask students to focus on ideas that address real-life climate issues or contribute to protecting the environment. Local businesspeople or community leaders volunteer as dragons. During or after the presentation, the dragons quiz teams on their ideas and challenge aspects of their business plans. Team members must demonstrate their knowledge and preparation by answering questions cogently. The dragons provide each team with constructively critical feedback.

Task

- Create a groupwork task for your students, based on problem-based learning. If possible, link the task to sustainability.
- Include in the task design opportunities for collaboration, presentations and peer and/or external feedback.
- Incorporate an opportunity for students to evaluate critically their team-working skills.

One-to-one teaching

In *The Voice*, *Strictly Come Dancing* and *Dancing on Ice*, the participants all benefit from one-to-one teaching from an expert in singing, dancing and skating, respectively. Working directly with their students in this way, teachers can start from where the student is at. Putting assessment for learning into practice, they get a really good sense of each student's strengths, weaknesses and progression and so understand what the student needs most to move forward.

Teachers' enthusiasm for their discipline, and their overt desire to help their students make progress, plays a significant role in effective teaching (Harper, 2013). This is very evident in the reality TV programmes where mentors work on a one-to-one basis with participants. It is, of course, easier for teachers if students are highly motivated. For example, talking about winning *Strictly Come Dancing*, Bill Bailey explained how he and his teacher, Oti Mabuse, worked together:

> *You think on the face of it we'd have not much in common. You know, we're different ages, different generations, different upbringings, countries, languages. But what we found we had in common was we have this kind of mutual respect for hard work. I'm quite competitive. I don't want to give a poor account of myself. If I leave the show, it won't be because I haven't practised, it'll be because I'm no good at it, but I'm going to give it my all. She took that as a challenge.*
>
> (Barr, 2023)

Task

○ Thinking back to the previous chapter, and the work of Carole Dweck (2006), what can you say about Bill Bailey's mindset from this quotation?

With these reality TV shows, there are no summative assessment criteria or examinations to pass, and once the TV programme ends, participants return to their normal life. It is different, of course, for FE students who need to meet a required standard to gain their qualification(s).

Apprentices benefit from one-to-one support from a mentor, as do teacher trainees in the workplace. FE teachers rarely have the luxury of timetabled sessions for one-to-one teaching, but in practical classes they are usually able to dedicate some time to each student as they walk around, observing how students are progressing. FE teachers also undertake tutorials with students.

Tutorials

One-to-one tutorials serve different purposes. *Academic* tutorials focus on a student's progress in their main subject(s). *Professional* tutorials may relate, for example, to general careers advice, job or placement applications or the drafting of a curriculum vitae. *Pastoral* tutorials address issues such as students' health and well-being or transport or financial concerns that may be adversely affecting their attendance and their studies.

In practice, these boundaries often blur, and tutors find themselves tackling all three aspects within one tutorial. Teachers need to be mindful of the limits to their expertise and of certain boundaries. Therefore, in some cases, they will direct students to the provider's specialist student support team, for example, for additional learning support or for specific health and well-being concerns.

The teaching method most commonly associated with effective one-to-one teaching and tutoring is *coaching*. There are different models of coaching but, in effect, it is generally recognised to mean that teachers do not attempt to solve students' problems but work with them to identify obstacles and support them to think about how they might overcome these. In doing so, teachers use techniques such as active listening (fully concentrating on what the student is saying), summarising and paraphrasing. They ask open questions and focus on goal setting, as well as ensuring that either they or the student keep a record of agreed actions.

Task

o   Identify a one-to-one tutorial you have participated in, as either teacher or student. To what extent did the coaching model apply, as described above?

3.6 INTEGRATING THEORY, ENGLISH AND MATHEMATICS

Theory

Knowledge and skills are inextricably linked, as discussed in the previous chapter. In *Big Dreams, Small Spaces*, as the enthusiasts take on the task of planning and creating their garden, they develop a greater understanding of basic plant and soil science. Without drawing on this knowledge in the early phase, their garden may not thrive in the longer term. In *The Great British Bake Off*, a lack of understanding of fermentation in bread making can result in a loaf having an unsatisfactory taste, size or texture. In these and other reality TV programmes, 'theory' is integrated into the sessions. There are no separate TV shows on how theoretical knowledge underpins the skills that participants are developing.

In FE, vocational teachers embed theory into their skills lessons as authentically as they can. For example, one student on a sports and exercise course observes a practical training session rather than participates due to an ankle sprain. With the student's permission, the teacher seizes this opportunity to refer to the injury and to widen the discussion about sports injuries in general with the whole group, even though this topic is usually covered in a separate theory session.

Theory lessons are usually necessary to ensure coverage of the curriculum. Making these sessions sufficiently interesting and relevant can be a challenge, as students may be less motivated than they are in practical sessions, and therefore less willing to attend and participate in activities. At first, it may be necessary to tap into students' *extrinsic* motivation to gain their qualification, as discussed in the previous chapter. Students tend to learn more readily if they are aware of the benefits for them of putting energy into their learning. For this reason, it is useful for the teacher to address explicitly the question they may be asking: '*What's the point of this?*'

Answering this question may necessitate contextualising the content so that students see its relevance to their practical skills and/or their future career. Simply providing students with information is not enough. Information can be downloaded to phones and computers, shown to students in a presentation, put on posters around the room, outlined in a lecture or given out to each student in a handout. However, it is of little or no value until students *do* something with it.

Teachers can help students to learn with activities and tasks that enable them to *apply* the information or analyse it some other way, such as comparing it to something else. The teacher's role is also to help students make sense of what they are learning and to give them timely, constructive feedback on what they have done with the information. Skilled teachers encourage students to deepen their knowledge by explaining to others what they have learned and assessing their own work and/or that of their peers. In theory lessons, with sufficiently challenging and relevant activities, opportunities to participate and reflect, and ongoing feedback, students are more likely to become intrinsically motivated to succeed and less likely to think about misbehaving or not co-operating.

Task

- If possible, use a digital polling tool in one of your lessons to ask students just two questions: firstly, how much do you enjoy practical classes on a scale of 1 to 5 (5 being very much) and, secondly, how much do you enjoy theory classes?
- Show students the summary of the responses and discuss with them the outcome of this survey.

English and mathematics

A *Dragons' Den* activity is an excellent context in which to develop students' speaking, listening and writing skills. Students can practise presenting ideas persuasively, taking into consideration the audience, purpose and context, as well as the formality and complexity of the language. They may also be able to compare this with the language used in professional kitchens, drawing on one or more of the many TV food shows.

Mathematical skills feature in many TV programmes, as highlighted in the previous chapter. There are plenty of mathematical concepts and skills to discuss in *The Great British Bake Off.* Hazel Lewis (2016) suggests those shown in Table 3.2.

Table 3.2 Mathematics in The Great British Bake Off

Division	Dividing cake mixture.
Fractions	For example, take ¾ of the cake mixture.
Formulae	There is a formula for making the correct number of layers.
Engineering skills	Using volume and area constructions for the showstoppers.
Scaling ratios	Adapting quantities in the recipe.
Time calculations	Particularly complex if baking different components.
Measurement	Using scales, measuring jugs and thermometers.

(Adapted from Lewis, 2016)

In FE, there is no one model when it comes to helping students who are on vocational courses to develop their knowledge and skills in English and mathematics. These may also be referred to as functional skills or literacy and numeracy. If teachers are required to *embed* these skills as part of their day-to-day teaching, they may need to update their own knowledge and skills. FE providers usually opt for one of the following models:

o embedded English and mathematics to be integrated into skills-based sessions, taught by the vocational teacher;

o embedded sessions, taught by the skills teacher, but with the additional support of a specialist English and/or mathematics teacher;

o discrete English and mathematics lessons, taught by specialists in these subjects, for each cohort to run alongside their main studies;

o English and mathematics lessons, taught by specialists in these subjects, for students on different courses in the same institution, allocated according to level rather than vocational discipline.

Task

o Which one, if any, of these models applies to your workplace or placement provider? If none of these, explain the model used.

o In your teaching, how do you promote and embed English and mathematics? Give specific examples.

3.7 TECHNOLOGY

Technology in the curriculum

While the look and format of some reality TV programmes, such as *University Challenge*, *QI* or *Mastermind*, has not changed for decades, many others now look very different, with gigantic screens, pulsing lights, flashing consoles and glowing floor panels.

The availability and relatively low cost of this technology has had an impact on all professions and skills, including teaching.

Your Home Made Perfect is one of many home improvement reality TV programmes, but it is different to others in that the presenter uses virtual reality (VR) to show people what their dream homes would look like before they undergo construction in real life. In each episode the homeowners, who state their budget, are uncertain about the way forward in renovating their house. Two architects come up with different plans. The homeowners choose the design they prefer, and construction work commences.

State-of-the-art technology in wildlife and nature documentaries gives viewers spectacular and unprecedented insight into life on our planet. *Frozen Planet II* is a documentary series about the world's coldest regions and how various species overcome challenges to endure its extreme environment. In this series the team commandeer satellites to capture images from space. They use high-definition remote camera traps, long-term time-lapse cameras and rebreather diving technology and pole cameras. They also use a range of drones: light-weight drones to give an aerial perspective; GPS-programmed drones to fly specific routes multiple times to capture changes in the landscape over time; high-speed first-person-view 'racer' drones to fly down mountains alongside avalanches; and thermal drones to follow pumas hunting at night (Considine, 2023).

Task

- Reflecting on Professional Standard 8: '*Develop and update knowledge of your subject specialism, taking account of new practices, research and/or industry requirements*', outline how you are keeping up to date, particularly in relation to current and emerging technologies.
- Think about the impact of this on how you prepare your students for the workplace.
- Use one of the available artificial intelligence applications to ask this question: *What are the latest technological developments in [add your subject or occupation here, for example: construction]*?
- How satisfied are you with the response? If possible, try the question again with a different artificial intelligence application.

Digital tools to support teaching and learning

FE providers invest in technology for three distinct purposes: to incorporate into the curriculum so that students learn relevant workplace skills; to support the management, administration and security of the organisation; and to enhance teaching and learning.

In *Your Home Made Perfect* and *Frozen Planet II*, the technology makes possible the seemingly impossible. In a home improvement programme, participants could look at models, drawings and diagrams, but with VR they experience walking around their new home. In wildlife programmes such as *Frozen Planet II* the drones give an aerial perspective on animal behaviour in situations where other aerial filming would have been too disturbing to wildlife or logistically unachievable.

In the same way, technology gives teachers considerable opportunities to enhance their students' learning. As with any resource or activity, what is important when using digital tools is the expertise of the teacher in deciding when and how to use them to support or assess learning. As noted earlier, virtual and augmented reality can bring complex subject matter to life and keep students engaged. Most significantly, it can be used across many technical areas to simulate potentially fatal scenarios without compromising students' safety.

FE teachers may not yet have routine access to satellites, robots and drones to support their teaching, but there are many digital tools that are readily available. They include applications that enable live polling, question and answer, word cloud creation, collation of ideas and general quizzing. Teachers and students can easily create presentations and record instructional videos and they can communicate through video calls or chats. Groups can collaborate on notes and designs, drawing on real-time data.

Robots have been commonplace in factories for many decades. Increasingly, they are used in care homes, for physical care and, more controversially, to provide interaction, companionship and emotional support. In education, post-pandemic, both teachers and students have become familiar with hybrid learning, whereby some students attend their studies in person while others join virtually. This has its challenges, as the teacher needs to plan carefully how they will engage and integrate virtual and classroom-based students.

Telepresence robots solve these problems to an extent. They allow students to attend classes remotely from home or elsewhere, using a robotic 'body' to represent them in the physical classroom. Students have control of the robot. They can drive the robot over to join a small group, and they can press a button to turn on flashing lights to indicate a raised hand. As they can contribute and listen, they are able to participate in group discussions. Telepresence robots, like any other technology, can be a form of assistive technology, with the potential to surmount barriers for people with disabilities.

Task

- Reflect on Professional Standard 16: '*Select and use digital technologies safely and effectively to promote learning*'. Identify one digital tool you routinely use and explain how it enhances learning for your students.

- Investigate digital tools you have not yet tried out and select one to use with your students. After the session, reflect on how effective it was in terms of teaching and learning.

3.8 CONCLUSION

There is no one-size-fits-all approach to teaching. As experienced teachers will attest, the same lesson plan applied to two different groups will turn out very differently. Every single lesson is unique and contingent on the professional judgement of the teacher in that particular setting, at that time, and with that particular student or group of students. Teachers provide structured opportunities for students to learn, and they assess this learning. With skills-based courses, this is to measure not just students' understanding but what students can do, produce or create as a consequence of that understanding. The different ways in which teachers assess learning are explored in the next chapter.

REFERENCES

Barr, S (2023) Bill Bailey Felt 'Riled' by 'Unflattering' Remarks about Him on Strictly Come Dancing before His Victory. *Metro*, 3 July. [online] Available at: https://metro.co.uk/2023/07/03/strictly-come-dancing-bill-bailey-riled-by-unflattering-remarks-19055690 (accessed 11 February 2024).

Biggs, J (1999) *Teaching for Quality Learning at University*. Buckingham: Society for Research into Higher Education and Open University Press.

Commission on Adult Vocational Teaching and Learning (2013) *It's about Work… Excellent Adult Vocational Teaching and Learning*. Coventry: Learning and Skills Improvement Service.

Considine, P (2023) [online] Frozen Planet II: All About the Technology. [online] Available at: https://www.televisual.com/news/frozen-planet-ii-allabout-the-technology/ (accessed 11 February 2024).

Dweck, C S (2006) *Mindset: The New Psychology of Success*. Random House.

Education and Training Foundation (2022) *Professional Standards for Teachers and Trainers*. [online] Available at: www.et-foundation.co.uk/professional-standards/teachers (accessed 11 February 2024).

Freire, P (2017) *Pedagogy of the Oppressed*. London: Penguin Random House.

Harper, H (2013) *Outstanding Teaching in Lifelong Learning*. Milton Keynes: Open University Press.

Lewis, H (2016) 9 Maths Skills You Need to Win the Great British Bake Off. [online] Available at: www.mathscareers.org.uk/9-maths-skills-bake-off (accessed 11 February 2024).

Lucas, B (2014) *Vocational Pedagogy: What It Is, Why It Matters and What We Can Do About It*. Report of the UNESCO-UNEVOC online conference, 12–26 May 2014.

Orr, K (2018) Getting Started: Gatsby Charitable Foundation. [online] Available at: www.improvingtechnicaleducation.org.uk/teacher-education/resources-library/getting-started (accessed 11 February 2024).

Orr, K, Hanley, P, Hepworth J and Thompson R (2019) *Enhancing Subject-specialist Pedagogy through the Initial Teacher Education of Science, Engineering and Technology Teachers in Further Education Colleges*. [online] Available at: https://pure.hud.ac.uk/en/publications/enhancing-subject-specialist-pedagogy-through-the-initial-teacher (accessed 11 February 2024).

Robson, J (2006) *Teacher Professionalism in Further and Higher Education: Challenges to Culture and Practice*. Abingdon: Routledge.

Shulman, L (1987) Knowledge and Teaching: Foundations of the New Reform. *Harvard Educational Review*, 57(1): 1–22.

4 Assessment

4.1 INTRODUCTION

In section 4.2 the purposes of assessment are considered, which are for initial assessment; to give feedback on learning; to give feedback on progress in learning; for summative assessment; and to test participants' potential to progress further beyond the end of the course. Section 4.3 looks at planning for assessment, including the key features and principles of assessment as well as initial assessment, while section 4.4 considers assessment strategies under five headings: tests and challenges; active assessment strategies; peer and self-assessment; evidence-based assessment; and extended assessment. Lastly, section 4.5 considers the quality assurance of assessment.

4.2 THE WHY: PURPOSES OF ASSESSMENT

Task

- Consider the range of assessments that you have used with your students or which you have undertaken as a student yourself. How many different purposes did those assessments serve?

Some assessments could have been used for the *selection and admission* of students for an appropriate course. The interview is often a key selection strategy for those responsible for admitting students to colleges, for example, particularly on courses for which there are threshold entry requirements. You could have been subjected to *initial assessment* before your course began or in its early stages. Such initial assessment would aim to help you and those responsible for your learning to be aware of your ability and potential; any prior learning or achievement; specific learning needs; personal interests; and professional skills such as reliability, self-confidence and problem-solving ability. Assessment can be used to *give feedback* both on *learning* and on *progress in learning*, as discussed in Chapter 3. It can be used *summatively*, as in the end-point assessment of apprenticeships, to test whether a candidate has the knowledge, skills and behaviours to cross a threshold. And assessment can test for the student's potential to *progress further beyond the end of a course*.

Task

- Watch a heats episode of *MasterChef* early in a series. Consider in this episode (and, if necessary, further episodes in the series) how judges or competitors themselves use assessment for the purposes outlined above.

- Specifically, which of the following apply?

    - for initial assessment;
    - to give feedback on learning;
    - to give feedback on progress in learning;
    - summatively;
    - to test participants' potential to progress further beyond the end of the programme.

We do not know from the programme itself how participants have been selected but this extract from SquareMeal gives an indication:

> It's actually all very simple. When entries reopen you will be able to fill out an application form from the official MasterChef website. Expect questions on your favourite chefs and what dishes you like to cook. You may also be asked about your culinary influences so get thinking about those early inspirational moments in the kitchen!
>
> You will need to provide a photograph and there is even opportunity to submit a video too if you want to show off your natural TV credentials! In previous years there have been phone interviews too.
>
> Once your application has been reviewed, producers will invite any successful candidates to interview. At this round, contestants are typically filmed while presenting to two of the show's producers. Each hopeful chef is required to bring a dish with them, which will have to be served cold. The team assure us they're used to imagining your dish hot – if it's supposed to be eaten so – but we suppose making something which does well at room temperature could only be a bonus. Expect to chat through the dish as well as answering other questions during your few minutes in the hot seat: they're after someone who can multitask with a camera in their face.
>
> (Mitchell, 2020)

4.3 THE WAY: PLANNING FOR ASSESSMENT

Key features of assessment

Assessment can be *formal or informal*. Perhaps the most formal kind of assessment would be an exam or a driving test. Formal assessment takes place as an organised, official occasion or event. In contrast, informal assessment takes place in informal situations: maybe an art tutor nodding positively while looking at your painting or a friend deliberately not laughing at your joke. In *The Great British Bake Off*, informal feedback is given as the judges wander around while the participants are baking and make comments about what they see.

Assessment can be *subjective or objective*. The phrase 'There's no accounting for taste' picks out the key feature of subjective assessment. Two of us stand in front of a painting. One says, '*I rather like that*'. You say, '*Not my kind of thing, really*'. There is no dispute here. Two different views. The views and the assessment are subjective. In contrast, there can be nothing more objective than a multiple-choice test: one right answer to one question. In fact, multiple-choice tests are often termed 'objective tests'.

Assessment can be *formative or summative*. Formative assessment 'forms' or supports learning and is usually applied during the learning process, while summative assessment 'sums up' achievement and takes place at the end of a learning process, whether that be a lesson, unit, module or course. *Continuous assessment* is an ongoing process during learning: continuous assessment need not be formative – it can simply assess or test learning rather than support it, a process more for the teacher's rather than the learner's benefit. *Terminal assessment* takes place at the end of a learning process and is usually the key assessment strategy of that process. End-point assessment at the end of an apprenticeship is an example of this.

Finally, there is a distinction between assessment of a *learning process* and *the product* of learning. The former would focus on the sourcing of ingredients and the cooking process, while the latter would be made at the tasting of the dish. In mathematics, for example, marks are often given for the method used to work out the solution to a problem, as well as for the right answer.

Task

- Review the *MasterChef* programme you viewed earlier. Can you find examples of all the key features of assessment?

Key principles of assessment

Choosing your yardstick

There are many TV programmes with a similar format, whereby each week one participant is selected by judges/experts to leave the competition. This weekly eviction helps to maintain drama and viewing figures, as discussed in Chapter 2. Such programmes include *RuPaul's Drag Race*, *The Great British Bake Off*, *The Great Pottery Throw Down*, *Interior Design Masters*, *Glow Up: Britain's Next Make-Up Star* and many more.

Task

- Watch an episode from any of these programmes and consider the different basis, yardstick or measuring tool used when making judgements about:
  - which participant should leave after a given round;
  - the level of achievement an individual has reached at any point in the competition;
  - the qualities individuals are presenting to the judges after a given round;
  - the participants' own development through the competition.

Norm referencing

Imagine that Gareth Malone, the TV choirmaster, asked each of you as an individual in a group to sing the verse of a song. After all the verses have been sung, he points at individuals and says: '*You were the best and you were second best. Yours was less strong and yours was middling*', and so on. He would be comparing individual performances with those of other members of the group or using the yardstick of *norm referencing*. The idea here is that the performances of any given group follow a normal curve of distribution, small percentages achieving high and low scores, with most achieving average scores.

So, in identifying the chef who has to leave, *MasterChef* judges use norm referencing. They have to agree on which chef over any given round, or rounds, has given the weakest (or least good) performance. This is why, when all performances turn out to be difficult to separate in terms of quality, norm-referenced judgements seem unpalatable ('*We had to make a decision – one of you had to go!*').

When applied to educational contexts, norm referencing has its strengths and weaknesses. On the one hand, it demonstrates an individual's performance in relation to that of their peers. On the other, any individual might find themselves higher or lower in any given group. Critics of norm referencing argue that it tells you nothing about the learning achievement of an individual, particularly in relation to any absolute, objective standards.

Grade referencing

Gareth now asks you all to sing another verse of the song. This time he says the following after each of you performs: '*Your performance was a 2, yours a 1, while yours was an 8 and yours a 10*'. We could equally say: '*Yours was B, yours B+, A for yours, C- for yours*'. In this case, he is using *grade referencing*, in the former case using numerical grades and, in the latter, using letters or literal grades. In cooking programmes, judges rarely use actual grades when assessing competitors' efforts, numerical or literal. However, they do describe levels or standards of achievement: *'That soufflé was very, very good but the chocolate brownies ... divine!'* Other competitive shows use numerical grade referencing, such as *Strictly Come Dancing* and *Dancing on Ice*.

Criterion referencing

Another verse of the song. This time, after an individual performance, Gareth comes to his judgement as follows: *'Your pitch was absolutely perfect and your enunciation crisp and clear. The verse was sung with powerful feeling and your phrasing conveyed the meaning of the verse'*. This time, he is using specific aspects of your singing to characterise and measure your performance. These aspects are criteria for appraisal and our yardstick this time is *criterion referencing*.

Criterion and grade referencing

Let's consider judgements made in *Dancing on Ice* and the scoring section of the *Eurovision Song Contest* final. In both cases, judges use grade referencing: 0–10 in *Dancing on Ice* and a distribution of points to competitors of up to 12 in *Eurovision*. After the grade assessment, each judge in *Dancing on Ice* is asked to explain this score and give their reasons, in other words, the criteria for their grade. Although some share common criteria, lift quality or balance, for example, each judge has their own subjective criteria. So, criterion referencing is often combined with grade referencing when levels of different criteria are matched with points on a scale. Indeed, this approach to referencing is often used as the basis for much assessment in skills-based courses, as illustrated in Table 4.1.

Table 4.1 An example of criterion and grade referencing for singing

GRADE → CRITERION ↓	A	B	C	D
Enunciation	Entirely crisp, clear	Largely clear with odd words difficult to understand	Some clarity of enunciation	Largely incomprehensible
Emotion	Powerfully rendered	Many passages of emotional expression	Patches of emotional expression	Emotionally flat
Phrasing	Varied phrasing clearly expresses meaning and gives style	Overall, clear expressive phrasing but, at times, out of sync with meaning	Phrasing simplistic or formulaic	Little phrasing

Ipsative referencing

Another verse please? Gareth then sits down with each of you and discusses your progress (or regress) or how well you have performed the verse compared with the last time you sang it. Making a judgement about this would be to use *ipsative referencing*, comparing one performance by an individual with a previous performance by the same individual. Athletes will often use ipsative referencing when monitoring their own career (*'well below my best time!'*). Participants on *Strictly Come Dancing* who survive the first few weeks of the competition routinely look back on their performance in the early shows and marvel at their own progress. If you are a teacher training student, you and your mentor or you and your tutor are likely to be using ipsative assessment on a regular basis to track your progress on the programme.

Task

- Consider your own experiences of using or being the subject of norm, grade, criterion and ipsative referencing. What were the positive and negative aspects of these experiences?

Validity

A valid assessment is one which assesses what it claims to assess. So the use of a written assessment to test if a plumbing student can install a hot water system would be an invalid use of that assessment. Notice that it is the suitability of the assessment strategy for judging whether the aims and outcomes of learning have been met which determines validity. Whereas a short-answer oral test for English for speakers of other languages (ESOL) might be sufficiently valid to judge English *comprehension*, it would require something like a full conversation in English to determine *fluency* in English. There are also gradations or degrees of validity: whereas the standard driving test might determine sufficient driving competency to gain a full licence, it is widely recognised that this is only partly valid as an assessment of the level of competency several years of driving might result in.

A valid assessment would also be one which ensured all the learning outcomes and curriculum content of a learning unit were covered. In addition, the high predictive validity of an assessment would guarantee that such assessment was a strong indicator of future achievement. So those developing an apprenticeship need to ensure that its end-point assessment has high validity as a predictor of future vocational competence.

Reliability

The reliability of an assessment strategy relates to the consistency with which it validly measures achievement. This consistency might be established through monitoring the achievement by different groups taking the same assessment or by the results reached by different assessors marking the same assessment. Reliability can be enhanced by clear, unambiguous performance criteria, detailed marking schemes and thorough moderation, verification and standardisation procedures (see section 4.5).

Task

o Rate the potential use of the assessment strategies in Table 4.2 for their validity and reliability from 1–5, where 5 is high and 1 is low.

Table 4.2 Task to rate assessment strategies for validity and reliability

Learning	Assessment strategy	Validity	Reliability
Knowing Spanish irregular verb forms	Conversation with native Spanish speaker		
Changing the washer on a tap	Observation by plumbing apprenticeship mentor		
Demonstrating product knowledge with a customer	Short-answer question test		
Trainee police officer understanding and applying the law on trespass	Essay		
Knowing how to cook a good cheese soufflé	Reciting a recipe word for word		
Describing *Hamlet's* emotional and psychological journey through the play	Essay		
Basic understanding of the roles of the executive, legislature and judiciary in the British constitution	Short-answer test		
Learning how to control student behaviour	Taking a multiple-choice test		
How to build a brick wall	Photographic display of the finished wall		
Effective use of perspective in drawing	Still-life painting		
Subject pedagogical knowledge	Written assignment		

Authenticity and practicability

An authentic assessment is one which has maximum capacity to ensure the work being assessed is that of the student themselves. This is clearly not a problem in TV skills-based programmes, where participants are seen dancing, sewing, baking or throwing pots. However, it has become an issue in education with the availability of artificial intelligence systems and, particularly in higher education, where assessment strategies often focus on written tasks. Authenticity also relates to the assessment setting: dismantling and reassembling an engine in a college motor vehicle workshop is more authentic than looking at a diagram in a classroom, but not as authentic as dismantling and reassembling a car engine in a garage. The practicability of an assessment is mainly related to whether the resources exist to be able to carry out the assessment properly: space, equipment, time, assessing staff.

Planning an assessment framework

Assessment planning is rarely carried out as a separate task in institutions but will often be part of a wider curriculum planning process. This might be the validation of a new programme, course or unit in HE or turning awarding organisation specifications into schemes of work and then session plans in FE.

John Biggs (Biggs et al, 2022) developed the term *constructive alignment*, as mentioned in Chapter 3, to describe the process in which appropriate teaching and learning activities are designed to enable students to meet learning outcomes, themselves clear statements about what students will be able to do by the end of a session, unit or course. These should then be aligned with assessment strategies which accurately measure whether such learning outcomes have been achieved.

Task

- Aims, learning outcomes and learning activities have been aligned in Table 4.3 but assessment strategies have been allocated at random. Align assessment strategies with appropriate aims and learning activities.

Table 4.3 Task to align assessment strategies with appropriate aims and learning activities

Aims	Learning outcomes (not exhaustive)	Learning activities	Assessment strategies
1. To communicate effectively with individuals, their families, carers and healthcare practitioners	• Show empathy. • Make yourself understood. • Explain instructions. • Accurately record conversations.	• Role play client conversation with tutor and take feedback on board.	a) Observation of session with client
2. To effectively direct the performance of a short scene of a play	• Show awareness of a range of lighting effects on the stage. • Show awareness of the range of sound effects available to them. • Communicate sympathetically with actors. • Direct actors with an understanding of the spatial relationships between them.	• Play going. • Interviewing directors. • Interviewing actors.	b) Assessment of record of achievement

Aims	Learning outcomes (not exhaustive)	Learning activities	Assessment strategies
3. To serve a customer effectively	• Demonstrate comprehensive product knowledge. • Exhibit active listening skills. • Appreciate customer needs.	• Search for strengths and drawbacks of different products in *Which?* • Engage in mock sales events.	c) Observation of performance
4. To direct effectively a full civil emergency rehearsal	• Direct the management team firmly. • Ensure lines of communication are clear and open. • Prepare alternative strategies to deal with unexpected events.	• Develop and communicate a clear plan of action. • Practise using communication channels.	d) Accompanied home visit to client
5. To drive a vehicle safely	• Anticipate upcoming road hazards. • Demonstrate 360° awareness around vehicle. • Drive at appropriate speed for road and conditions. • Drive with care and avoid risks.	• Driving lessons. • Trips with a qualified friend.	e) Filmed or videoed event
6. To boil and serve an egg	• Use of an accurate timing mechanism. • Has ensured eggs are at an appropriate temperature to avoid cracking before immersion. • Produced an egg yolk as requested by consumer.	• Study recipe. • Practise egg boils.	f) Observation of service of a customer
7. To conduct TV interviews effectively	• Put subject at ease. • Ask answerable questions. • Ask follow-up questions which lead to amplification and development.	• Practise interview with feedback.	g) Appraisal of performance/ interview audience
8. To be able to support clients in expressing their emotions	• Demonstrate sympathy. • Draw out client's feelings with sensitivity. • Respond to client's expression.	• Relevant reading. • Observe counsellor/ client sessions.	h) Simulation

Aims	Learning outcomes (not exhaustive)	Learning activities	Assessment strategies
9. To be able to give positive feedback	• Accurate use of critical terms. • Realistic feedback. • Offering of alternative strategies for improvement.	• Experience of other demonstrations of activity or performance. • Observation of effective feedback.	i) Extensive driving test
10. To monitor own progress	• Measure achievement against targets. • Recognise areas for improvement. • Honest about own achievement.	• Consistent recording of achievement. • Noting any critical feedback.	j) Consume prepared food

Suggested alignment: 1d, 2g, 3f, 4h, 5i, 6j, 7e, 8a, 9c, 10b

○ Choose a programme you are currently teaching. Examine the programme scheme of work and complete the following checklist.

- How appropriately and comprehensively do the learning outcomes meet the aims?
- How well do the learning activities specified help students achieve the learning outcomes? Are there additional learning activities that might help do this?
- How well do the assessment strategies measure fulfilment of the learning outcomes?
- How valid, reliable, authentic and practicable are the assessment strategies?

Initial assessment

Locate a heats episode of *MasterChef or MasterChef: The Professionals* early in a series when competitors were making their initial dishes or were having to recook to gain a coveted apron.

One test used frequently in *MasterChef: The Professionals* is *The Skills Test*. This involves one of the experts preparing quite a straightforward dish with simple ingredients out of sight of the competitors. One by one, the competitors are given the name of the dish, the ingredients and a time limit and asked to create the dish.

Task

- To what extent do you think this initial assessment is appropriate in a competition for *professionals*?

This gives the presenters the opportunity to see if participants are, as they should be, *already* beyond the threshold of a level of professional skills. Interestingly, nerves often get the better of seasoned chefs cooking for the first time in a TV studio and they can blow the task, sometimes not finishing and other times omitting key ingredients, so there is a degree of leniency in assessment. Nevertheless, it gives the judges a taste (as it were) of each participant's potential.

Another early test used in *MasterChef* has been *The MasterChef Invention Test*. Here, an extensive variety of all manner of foods is given to participants to choose ingredients with the brief that they cook whatever they like: '*it could be whatever you want it to be*'.

Some of the comments made by participants during this test indicate they know what the judges are after:

> *I'm really going to try and put my personality into my food – that's what I want them to see today.*

> *I tend to do mood food really – whatever I'm in the mood for.*

> *I love people. I'm a people pleaser*

> *[My style is] probably like Asian Fusion. I love taking dishes that I've eaten while I've been travelling. I've been to China, Hong Kong, The Philippines ...*

Task

- What is it about the judges' assessment criteria that these contestants understand?

One of the key aspects of a successful chef, particularly of those who go on to be star cooks, is their unique identity, the style, nature, hallmark of their cookery which no other chef possesses. In the early stages of the competition, this is what the judges are on the lookout for in each participant.

Task

- Choose something you're good at. It could be painting, playing the guitar, carpentry, singing, rapping. Try to describe your unique style or hallmark in doing this.
- In opening episodes of *The Apprentice*, candidates are interviewed as to why they would make a suitable business partner for Lord Sugar. If possible, watch

one of these episodes. Make a short video clip in which a friend interviews you and in which you have to convince the interviewer quickly why you, rather than other applicants, are suited to the course, teaching post or promotion you have applied for.

4.4 THE HOW: ASSESSMENT STRATEGIES

Tests and challenges

A test or challenge is the assessment strategy we are likely to be most familiar with and which, either positively or negatively, will be the most memorable: citizenship test, driving test(s), GCSEs, A levels, BTECs, degree exams, end-point assessment.

Task

- If you are not familiar with any of the following, watch an episode of *Mastermind*, *University Challenge*, *Tipping Point* or *Who Wants to Be a Millionaire?* In each of these there is questioning. What are the test conditions each programme has in common?

As a strategy, the test has at least three conditions: a usually formal controlled situation/environment in which participants have limited resources to help them, a tight time frame and single correct/incorrect answers or actions. In all four programmes, competitors are in a TV studio, usually in front of an audience. Questions are posed by an authoritative quizzer. There are a limited number of questions in a time frame and responses to these are themselves timed. Answers are usually brief and are closed – either correct or incorrect – in fact, the questions in *Mastermind* can be a lot longer than the answers.

The 'usually formal controlled situation/environment' need not be an exam room, in which knowledge tests, such as multiple-choice tests or essay papers, might be administered, nor a TV studio, in which most of our quiz TV shows take place. One episode of the *Race Across the World* series followed participants who were challenged to race across Canada, the largest country in the world, but the *conditions* under which they did this were closely controlled: no phones, no credit/bank cards, £50 each cash per day and the capacity to work to earn more. Resources available to contestants vary between programmes: *Who Wants to Be a Millionaire* contestants have *50:50, Phone a Friend* or *Ask the Audience*; *Who Wants to Be a Millionaire* contestants and those in the *Tipping Point* jackpot round have four and three possible answers to choose from, whereas *Mastermind* contestants have none. The limitation of and time constraints on questioning and answering and the closed questions are all in the interests of fairness and reliability.

Fairness in assessment is a key factor in inclusive teaching and learning. To some extent, assessment is fairer if the key principles of assessment, discussed above, are followed: validity, reliability, authenticity and practicability. However, fairness needs to be seen in a broader context:

> *We argue that 21st-century assessment will need to take ever more account of the social contexts of assessment and to continue the movement away from seeing fairness simply as a technical concern with test construction. Fairness in assessment involves both what precedes an assessment (for example, access and resources) and its consequences (for example, interpretations of results and impact) as well as aspects of the assessment design itself.*
>
> *How would we tell whether a test is fair for different groups (male/female; socially advantaged/disadvantaged; ethnic groupings)? The dilemma is that different groups will have different qualities and experiences, so fairness in assessment cannot be judged in terms of equal scores or outcomes.*
>
> (Gipps and Stobart, 2010, p 105)

These broader issues are discussed more fully in Chapter 5 on inclusion.

Task

- You have 10 minutes to complete the test in Figure 4.1. This tests what you have learned from section 4.2 about key features of assessment and key principles of assessment.
- What was your mark out of 10?
- Were you pleased, disappointed or surprised by this score?
- Did you have a response when you saw the phrase 'assessment test'?
- To what extent did you think this was a valid and reliable assessment of your understanding of the features and principles of assessment?

> *Was the test a valid and reliable assessment of your understanding of the features and principles of assessment? It could be argued that it was a valid test in that it tested understanding: you could not have filled in the gaps without understanding the key terms and applying them in contexts other than those in which you learned them. On the other hand, it could be argued that it was invalid in that it tested surface rather than deep learning. A more valid test of your deeper learning and understanding would have been for you to have constructed and administered your own assessment according to the features and principles you had learned, in other words, an active assessment strategy ...*
>
> (Armitage and Cogger, 2019, p 134)

> **Assessment test**
>
> COMPLETE THE GAPS
>
> 1. A .... assessment is one which actually measures what it claims to.
> 2. Assessing driving skills using a two-week open-book exam would be a/an .... method.
> 3. The more a technique allows for personal interpretation by the assessor, the less .... it becomes.
> 4. Assessment which occurs at intervals throughout the course is described as ....
> 5. Whereas exams are .... assessment strategies, open discussion is more ....
> 6. .... referencing compares the same student's previous performances with their present one.
> 7. Assessment concerned with players' accuracy with the ball and passing skills rather than on whether the team won would be focusing on ....
> 8. Relating an individual student achievement to that of the group they are a member of is known as .... referencing.
> 9. Giving a student a percentage mark would be to use .... referencing.
> 10. Cooking a restaurant-class dish in the *MasterChef* kitchen is more .... than cooking it in your own home but not as .... as cooking it in the restaurant kitchen itself.

Figure 4.1 Assessment test

Source: Armitage and Cogger, 2019

Answers: 1 valid, 2 invalid, 3 objective, 4 formative or continuous, 5 formal, informal, 6 ipsative, 7 process, 8 norm, 9 grade/numerical, 10 authentic

Active assessment strategies

Task

- If possible, watch an episode of *Race Across the World* on BBC iPlayer. What appear to be the key knowledge, understanding, abilities and skills the challenge is testing?

It is likely your answer to this task question will be focused on two broad areas: abilities and capacities on the one hand, which are often called personal or soft skills, and, on the other, communications and relationship skills. Active assessment strategies, such as a six-week trek, are ideal for assessing such abilities over a period of time in continually dynamic contexts. (Those of you who have completed the Duke of Edinburgh's Award Scheme – 323,000 young people in 2022–23 alone – will know that this involves a similar experience.)

In *Race Across the World*, the abilities and capacities participants need include both physical and emotional strength. They need to be resourceful, making the most of what they are given and can find. They need to be creative in their problem-solving, showing ingenuity in the way they overcome obstacles. They need to be resilient and unafraid of hard work. They need logistical ability and a capacity to spend wisely and budget carefully.

The testing of communications skills is complex. Participants are placed in pairs, each of which already has a long history: close friends, father–daughter, husband and wife, brothers. In this challenge, they are being asked to work in ways they probably never have before and we witness tensions between them. They have to learn to work collaboratively: teams fall out quickly about which route to take and get very emotional. We also see how dependent each will become on the other's mentoring skills, and see them experience other challenges of teamwork – knowing one another's strengths, listening and joint decision making.

Although participants' use of their abilities and communication skills are important factors in their experiences, for many the experience is life changing. You may have been surprised by the major changes in themselves and their lives the competition gave rise to. Many students who have experienced further or adult education testify to similar life changes as a result, which can be described as transformational. There is anecdotal evidence that many FE teachers are motivated to enter the profession as a result of such transformational experiences themselves as FE students. Smith and Duckworth (2022) report the experience of one such teacher, Eugene:

> *For me I think the most important thing it's probably the relationship with the student and I think that's because of my own journey … I have sat down and I've gone through my own journey myself on lots of occasions with the students … and even if it's stuff on the outside as well so if they've got problems on the outside of college, you know talk to them about that whatever it may be even if it's got nothing to do with college. It doesn't have to be just college and college work but looking or watching out for the person as an individual holistically.*
>
> (Smith and Duckworth, 2022, p 93)

Task

- Have you or any of your students experienced a similar transformative experience in your further or higher education?
- Watch an episode of *Dragons' Den*, if possible. The following active assessment strategies are used in the programme. Give examples of when they are used and explain how effectively you think they are used:

- role play;
- simulation;
- presentation/showcase;
- interview;
- problem-solving;
- questioning;
- discussion;
- professional dialogue;
- work-based assessment;
- creative arts/artefacts;
- panel discussion.

In the business world, those with products they have developed do not usually present their project to a panel of potential investors. The *Dragons' Den* interviews are therefore constructed for entertainment purposes, a simulation in which the dragons role play investors (even though they may turn out to be actual investors) and the guests role play presenters of their projects. This is a similar scenario to micro teaches you may have taken part in: you role play being a teacher, while your peers role play being your students. *Dragons' Den* participants are judged on their presentations, as well as the answers they give to the dragons as they are subsequently interviewed. In developing their projects and marketing strategies, participants will need to engage in creative problem-solving which the dragons will be keen to hear about. Questioning participants may take the form of a discussion or professional dialogue in which technical product matters, marketing and finance are discussed in what is a work-based context. Participants are judged on the niche they have identified for their artefact/product, and dragons will often sample the product for themselves and engage in panel discussion with each other in reaching a judgement.

Task

o Think about constructive alignment, described earlier. Now look at one of your schemes of work or lesson plans. Have you used any of the active assessment strategies considered in the previous task? If not, considering your learning aims, outcomes and learning activities, reflect on opportunities to use a wider range of strategies.

o Games are a good way of actively assessing knowledge, in particular. Watch an edition of *University Challenge*. The rules of the TV programme are set out below, but to create your own game, you can devise your own scoring system if you prefer. You may prefer to use one or more of the many electronic tools available to support tests and games. For example, you may set up the competition so that students can use their mobile phones to provide answers.

- One suggestion is to divide the larger group you teach into three sub-groups: 1, 2 and 3. Each group should develop a set of starter and bonus questions based on different areas of their subject (this is to ensure the different groups do not duplicate the questions of others). The tournament comprises three games:

  1. Gp 1 plays Gp 2, Quizzer from Gp 3 using Gp 3 questions.
  2. Gp 2 plays Gp 3, Quizzer from Gp 1 using Gp 1 questions.
  3. Gp 1 plays Gp 3, Quizzer from Gp 2 using Gp 2 questions.

- Following the tournament, what did you learn about using games as a form of assessment?

The rules of *University Challenge*

Questions begin in the form of starters for 10 points and must be answered on the buzzer with no conferring. The team that answers a starter correctly then gets three linked bonus questions for 5 points each during which the team may confer, with the captain (who sits third from the left) giving their final answer. If a contestant interrupts a starter question and answers incorrectly, his or her team loses 5 points (sometimes leading to negative scores) and the other side gets the whole question. There are also two picture and one music rounds during each show (5 points are lost for incorrectly interrupting the music starter). The actual game lasts around 26 minutes and is ended with the famous sound of a gong. If at the end the scores are level, the game is decided by a single tie break starter, with the winner being the first side to answer a starter correctly. However, if someone interrupts the tie break incorrectly, then their side loses 5 points, and they lose the game.

(Blanchflower, 2023)

It is likely that a lot of time and energy (and noise) was spent ensuring that the rules of the game were followed. And this indicates the central importance of *fairness* in assessment. Note the time, energy, noise and controversy involved when a penalty is awarded in professional football by the referee and/or video assessment referee (VAR).

Peer and self-assessment

In one episode of *Great British Menu* the expert sets out some of the assessment criteria: 'great technique', 'brilliant understanding of ingredients' and the chefs need to feature an illustration or an animation that inspired the dish. Once the dish is presented, the judge does not give his or her view but asks the chef to self-assess. After this, the chef's peers (and competitors) are asked for their views.

Task

- What, in your view, is the value of self-assessment and peer assessment of work, as opposed to expert assessment?

An important aspect of particularly professional and technical training and development is autonomy in working, performance and practice. Autonomy can only be developed if trainees can reflect on their practice, identify areas of strength as well as areas for development and follow strategies for improvement in those areas. Effective self-assessment is at the centre of this process, as discussed in Chapter 2 on learning.

If you are following a course for teaching in FE and skills, it is likely that you completed a micro-teach session early in the course. If so, you will know not only that peer assessors are honest in their appraisals but that they are extremely sympathetic towards their peers. This sympathy is not what a cynic might say is the need to scratch your back so you scratch theirs, but a genuine empathy and understanding of how difficult your achievement has been because of the requirement that they complete the same task. In episodes of *MasterChef*, *The Great British Bake Off* and *Great British Menu*, peers genuinely appreciate what it takes to achieve high quality because they are attempting to do so themselves.

Task

- Complete a self-assessment analysis regarding what you have learned about your own assessment practice from this chapter so far.
- What do you think are the strengths of your current practice?
- What are your weaknesses?
- What opportunities will there be to develop your practice?
- What challenges or threats to your future assessment practice do you foresee?

Evidence-based assessment

Evidence-based assessment is used widely in skills-based education. This involves the demonstration, through a range of evidence, that a student has reached a particular standard. There will be a specification of what evidence will be *sufficient* for this judgement to be made. Students taking the *Diploma in Teaching (Further Education and Skills)* must meet exactly the same standards as those completing the apprenticeship *Teaching Young People and Adults within all Parts of the Education and Training Sector*. The assessment of the Professional Practice module in the diploma is partly evidence based and presented in the Professional Practice portfolio:

- *The candidate must complete a portfolio of evidence relating to the placement[s] which is submitted to the module assessors.*

- The portfolio will feature a cross reference matrix demonstrating where the candidate has met the occupational standards in their professional practice, counter signed by their placement mentor/course tutor.

    (Education and Training Foundation, 2022, p 12)

The key elements of the Professional Practice module in the *Diploma in Teaching (Further Education and Skills)* are:

Unit 4: Professional Practice

Part A: Teaching practice

- Micro teaches
- Preparation for placement
- Observation of other teachers
- Team and solo teaching
- Curriculum planning and review
- Lesson planning and adaptations
- Planning and conducting assessment
- Using assessment to inform planning
- Assessment feedback and advice/guidance
- Application of evidence-based methods
- Managing and supporting learners including behaviour
- Placement log

Part B: Being A Professional

- The Occupational Standards
- Developing expertise
- Updating and CPD
- Professional responsibilities
- Working with colleagues
- Professional Status

Part C: The FE and Skills sector

- Overview of FE and Skills Sector
- Types of programmes
- Timetables
- Contracts

- Govt policy
- Regulations [legal and local]
- Funding
- Organizational and wider support

(Education and Training Foundation, 2022, pp 9–10)

Extended assessment

Assessment which takes place over an extended period gives students the opportunity to be assessed in more valid and reliable ways. This applies to complex work in higher education at levels 4+ with pieces of work such as the dissertation and thesis and is being increasingly used at levels 1–3 with project work, whether it be at GCSE, A level, T level, the International Baccalaureate and in apprenticeships at all levels.

Projects can take many forms, for example:

- research/enquiry;
- design and make – artefacts, works of art;
- portfolio;
- diary;
- case study;
- construction;
- manufacture;
- challenge/problem-solving;
- real-world/industry set projects;
- community based;
- family based;
- personal interest based;
- communication – blog, podcast, video, vlog.

Task

- Watch an edition of *DIY SOS: The Big Build* and consider the following questions about your episode.
    - Who set the project brief?
    - Were there any time constraints for the project and, if so, why were they applied?
    - How was the design of the build arrived at?

- Were there unforeseen problems and how were they resolved?
- Which construction skills most impressed you?
- Were there any technological developments which speeded work up?
- What motivates the workforce?
- Is there conflict between members of the workforce?
- How effectively did workers collaborate?
- How would you describe the team spirit of the workforce?
- How was the project assessed and who assessed it?

o Now design a project brief for your own students. You may, if you wish, use any project brief format of your awarding board/organisation but you will find most are a version of the following:

  - performance/learning outcomes/assessment criteria;
  - assessment arrangements regarding these including mark scheme and weightings;
  - the project brief – the context/scenario, details of the workplace if relevant, details of the consumer/customer/client and their needs and requirements, student role in this and the roles of others;
  - tasks, timings and checklist of evidence required;
  - (for T levels) details of the assessment of maths, English and digital skills.

4.5 QUALITY ASSURANCE OF ASSESSMENT

Standardisation is the process whereby assessors agree what qualities of a piece of work are required for the work to have achieved a particular standard. All the examiners for a GCSE paper, for example, might be sent an essay written by the same student and asked to mark it using the same rubric (groups of criteria) and mark scheme. They would then meet and discuss marks awarded, reaching a consensus on mark range and standards.

Moderation involves two or more assessors marking the same piece of work chronologically. This work is first marked by one assessor and then second marked by another (and sometimes third marked by another). The second or third marker will either blind mark (mark the work without seeing the first assessor's comments) or read the first assessor's comments before marking (in which case they can comment on the first assessor's feedback as well as the first assessor's judgement).

While moderation and standardisation are concerned with the accuracy of assessment in relation to standards, the *internal and external verifier* will be concerned with whether assessment practices and processes are operating fairly and consistently internal to the college or organisation or across colleges or organisations. In higher education, external verifiers are known as *external examiners* and both authors have extensive experience of this. Activities they have been involved in include meeting students to evaluate their course, observing or co-observing students teach with a tutor or mentor, and sampling work marked by different assessors or more than one piece of work by the same assessor.

Task

- What challenges to the standardisation, moderation and verification of work are there in the use of the following assessment strategies mentioned in this chapter?
    - self-assessment;
    - peer assessment;
    - six-week continent traverse;
    - projects such as *The Big Build*;
    - role play/simulation;
    - discussion;
    - presentation/showcase;
    - creative arts/artefacts;
    - work-based assessment;
    - professional dialogue;
    - interview;
    - panel discussion.

4.6 CONCLUSION

As we saw in Chapter 2, people learn in a variety of ways. Effective assessment involves understanding this and selecting from our repertoire of assessment strategies those which are most appropriate. To do this necessitates an understanding of validity, reliability, practicality and fairness. Equality and inclusion in assessment and in teaching will be addressed more fully in Chapter 5.

REFERENCES

Armitage, A and Cogger, A (2019) *The New Apprenticeships*. St Albans: Critical Publishing.

Biggs, J, Tang, C and Kennedy, G (2022) *Teaching for Quality Learning at University*. 5th ed. Maidenhead: McGraw-Hill/Open University Press.

Blanchflower (2023) University Challenge. [online] Available at: www.blanchflower.org/uc/index.html (accessed 11 February 2024).

Education and Training Foundation (ETF) (2022) *Diploma in Teaching (Further Education and Skills): Qualification Framework for the Full Teaching Qualification for the Further Education and Skills Sector.* London: ETF.

Gipps, C and Stobart, G (2010) Fairness in Assessment. In Wyatt-Smith, C and Cumming, J (eds) *Educational Assessment in the 21st Century: Connecting Theory and Practice* (pp 105–18). Dordrecht: Springer.

Institute for Apprenticeships and Technical Education (IfATE) (2019) *Teaching Young People and Adults within all Parts of the Education and Training Sector.* London: IfATE. [online] Available at: https://www.instituteforapprenticeships.org/apprenticeship-standards/learning-and-skills-teacher-v1-2 (accessed 11 February 2024).

Mitchell, E (2020) How to Apply for MasterChef: Everything You Need to Know. Squaremeal.co.uk, 9 January. [online] Available at: www.squaremeal.co.uk/restaurants/best-for/how-to-apply-for-masterchef_9561 (accessed 11 February 2024).

Smith, R and Duckworth, V (2022) *Transformative Teaching and Learning in FE: Pedagogies of Hope and Social Justice.* Bristol: Bristol University Press.

Inclusion, diversity and well-being

5.1 INTRODUCTION

This chapter tackles three inter-related themes: inclusion, diversity and well-being. Section 5.2 includes discussion of disability, inclusive teaching and neurodiversity. Following this, section 5.3 on diversity explores race and culture, gender, sexuality, social class and age, and then how different forms of discrimination intersect. This is followed by a discussion of the language associated with inclusion and diversity. The final section (section 5.4) explores issues relating to both student and staff well-being.

5.2 INCLUSION

FE has a long tradition of welcoming and teaching students of all abilities, ages and backgrounds. Stories abound across the whole sector of former students who have overcome difficult circumstances to succeed in their studies, seemingly against all the odds. Indeed, in the previous chapter, reference was made to the fact that many FE teachers are motivated to enter the profession as a result of their own transformational experiences as FE students.

Disability

The FE sector includes specialist colleges for young people with learning difficulties and/or disabilities (LDD). In addition, many general FE colleges provide education and training for students with LDD. Terms other than LDD include SEND (special educational needs and disabilities) and *high needs*, the latter of which is used by funding and inspection bodies.

The final of *Strictly Come Dancing* in 2021:

> ... briefly turned the sequin-heavy, primetime light-entertainment show into a deeply affecting, powerful platform for deaf visibility. Midway through the number, the music faded out. For 20-ish seconds, Ayling-Ellis and her partner, Giovanni Pernice, danced both in total silence and synchronicity. It was a fleeting insight into how Strictly's first deaf contestant experienced the show; a simple yet soul-stirring nod to the community she takes such pride in representing.
>
> (*The Guardian*, 2023)

In terms of learning a skill, the factors contributing to the success of Rose Ayling-Ellis were no doubt similar to those of other winners. She was highly motivated, worked hard, practised regularly, took on board feedback, made great progress and was popular with viewers who voted for her.

To provide the best environment for her to learn, the producers arranged deaf-awareness training for themselves, the cast and crew. Many learned British sign language (BSL), as did her teacher, Giovanni Pernice. He worked with his student to understand how she could learn the dance routines, and he adapted his teaching style, focusing on muscle memory more than music. An in-studio BSL interpreter was always on hand.

This approach to supporting people with disabilities so that they can engage meaningfully and achieve their full potential was not the first on reality TV. For example, in 2020 Libby Clegg, who is blind, came third in *Dancing on Ice*; Hollie Arnold, born without her right forearm, participated in *I'm a Celebrity*; and Amar Latif was the first blind contestant on *Celebrity Masterchef*. Inclusive learning and teaching, as reflected in these examples, is about respecting diversity and removing barriers to enable full participation.

Task

- What can teachers learn about inclusive teaching from the following two interview extracts?

Case study

Strictly Come Dancing

Rose Ayling-Ellis talks about her reaction to the ideas initially presented to her about the dance that in its final version on *Strictly Come Dancing* included a short period of total silence.

> 'I hated it,' Ayling-Ellis says ... 'I watched this pre-recorded video by external choreographers and immediately didn't like what they'd come up with. I was up for the idea, as long as it wasn't a patronising stunt. An attempt to get the pity vote, all sad, dreary and "poor me".' ... 'It was what hearing people think deaf people experience. Very insular, cut-off, small. It was so sad. And that's not me.' That routine was binned. Instead, with the help of other Strictly professionals, the couple reworked it, collaboratively. 'It felt totally different,' she says. 'From there, we created the dance, shaping and changing it throughout the week.' The result, she hoped, would be more energetic, more vibrant, more full of life. 'And most importantly,' she adds, 'more true to me.'
>
> (*The Guardian*, 2023)

> ## Case study
>
> ### *The Great British Bake Off*
>
> Briony Williams talks about her experience on *The Great British Bake Off*.
>
> **Did you ask the producers not to talk about your disability in the show or was it naturally not mentioned?**
>
> *I asked them not to mention my disability because I wanted to be treated like everyone else. I wanted to show people that even with my 'little hand', I could succeed. I just wanted it to happen organically, and for people to notice and then have that conversation, rather than making a big deal out of it. I wanted to be seen as one of the bakers, and not to be slapped with a big label from the beginning. I just wanted to go through on my own merit.*
>
> *The production team were great about it. We had a chat before I went into the tent and they asked if I needed any extra help and I said no.*
>
> *There should be more people representing disability on TV without us always having to talk about it. From disabled actors to presenters, we shouldn't have to focus on it or a disability topic. It should just be natural that we're there.*
>
> (Disability Horizons, 2020)

While the medical model of disability focuses on the fact that people have disabilities because of impairments or conditions, the social model suggests that disability is created by society. This is because too often people with disabilities face barriers that stop them from taking part in society in the same way as non-disabled people. Adjustments are used to retrofit. Individuals only need them because of an initial design that fails to take their needs into account. Research has shown that inclusive practices that embrace the social model and address societal barriers can improve academic achievement, social integration and self-esteem among students with disabilities (Ainscow, 2012; Hoole, 2023).

More contestants with disabilities taking part in TV reality and talent shows does not necessarily lead to less discrimination. However, there is an argument that this type of mainstream media is contributing to breaking down social and attitudinal barriers about people with disabilities by demonstrating what they *can* do. For example, Lost Voice Guy, real name Lee Ridley, is a stand-up comedian who won *Britain's Got Talent* in 2018. He has cerebral palsy and is unable to speak. He delivers his comic material through a text-to-voice application.

Text-to-speech software, available on smartphones and tablets, as used by Lost Voice Guy, is one of many assistive technologies used in education. Some of the technologies are hi-tech, costly and beyond the reach of the FE sector at present, such as the telepresence robots mentioned in Chapter 3. These enable individuals to be present and active in a remote physical space with a surrogate robot body. However, assistive technologies need not be that sophisticated or expensive. They can be any item, piece of equipment, software program or product that is used to improve life and learning for people with disabilities. For example, they may include clips that make it easier to turn pages. The important point is that to qualify as assistive, they must meet the individual student's needs.

Task

- Investigate provision for students with LDD in your placement or work institution and find out which assistive technologies are available and how they are used.

Inclusive teaching

Inclusive teaching is not just about teaching students with learning difficulties and/or disabilities. Regardless of subject, ability or level, every student is different and teaching inclusively enables them all to participate.

It may be difficult to get to know all of your students before you meet them, or even within the first few weeks, but it is still possible to plan, teach and assess inclusively. Teachers can:

1. offer a welcoming environment, particularly in the first few sessions, to encourage a sense of belonging;
2. ask students to suggest and agree their own ground rules;
3. plan teaching and assessment activities so that *all* students can participate;
4. encourage active learning;
5. provide timely formative feedback on students' contributions and use positive reinforcement, when appropriate, to acknowledge students' hard work and progress;
6. focus on students' strengths and interests rather than on a deficit model;
7. use diagnostic assessment and assessment for learning (AfL) to find out about students' prior knowledge, skills and experience, and to identify potential barriers to learning;
8. ask students who have declared a disability what they need, rather than assume that certain adjustments will work. This links back to the two interview excerpts above, where both Rose Ayling-Ellis and Briony Williams emphasise the importance of being asked what they need.

Task

- Think back to the first few weeks of:

    (a) a course you have participated in as a student;

    or

    (b) a course you have taught.

- To what extent was the teaching inclusive? How would you describe the atmosphere in the group? Did all students participate and make progress?
- If you think it *was* inclusive, what factors contributed to this? What might have made it more inclusive?

Neurodiversity

Neurodiversity refers to how everyone's brain develops and works in different ways, leading to differences in how people learn and experience the world around them. It is used as an umbrella term for conditions such as dyslexia, autism, dyspraxia, dyscalculia and attention deficit hyperactivity disorder (ADHD). The Centre for Neurodiversity at Work (C4NDAW) at Birkbeck, University of London, also includes within this overarching term learning disabilities, sensory processing disorder, anxiety and depression. Around one in seven people in the UK are believed to be neurodivergent (Faragher, 2023, p 15). In effect, it is difficult to estimate how many students (and staff) in FE are neurodivergent as not all symptoms are visible or diagnosed, and even if they are people may be reluctant to divulge this information.

The potential *physical* barriers for the TV reality show participants mentioned earlier are self-evident. However, not all barriers are visible. For example, it was not known when Nadiya Hussain appeared on *The Great British Bake Off* that she suffered from a panic disorder (Long, 2017), as mentioned in Chapter 2, and many other reality TV show participants have talked about mental health issues.

In FE, it is not uncommon for students to have hidden barriers to learning, particularly if they feel they failed at school. This applies to students progressing into FE directly from school, as well as to older students whose last educational experience may have been a long time ago. Students, for a range of reasons, may have a general dislike of teachers and authority figures. Undoubtedly, some will have a fixed mindset, as described in Chapter 2, and assume that learning is always boring or too difficult. This makes it even more important for FE teachers to create a positive and inclusive learning environment and to help students to gain confidence.

5.3 DIVERSITY

Students may also experience barriers in the form of other people's assumptions about their ability and potential because of their race, gender, religion, age, sexual orientation or class.

The extent to which reality TV programmes are diverse, in terms of participants, presenters, professionals and judges, is important. These programmes convey a message about the UK population today and whether certain activities, such as quizzing, dancing, skating, sewing, gardening or baking, are suitable for everyone. This, in turn, can have a powerful influence on raising awareness and changing attitudes.

For example, interest in BSL surged after Rose Ayling-Ellis joined *Strictly Come Dancing*. One report suggests that there was a 488 per cent spike in Google searches for BSL courses, and enrolment for one provider of BSL courses rose by 2000 per cent (K Ng, 2021). Against this backdrop of public interest in BSL, and more than a decade of campaigning by Rosie Cooper MP, in April 2022 a bill was passed to legally recognise BSL as an official language in England, Wales and Scotland.

Race and culture

Although *The Great British Bake Off* is usually associated with inclusivity and diversity, it has not been without controversy. It stopped its national-themed challenges after receiving criticism about 'Mexican week' in 2022. In the episode, the hosts wore sombreros, used maracas and spoke in accents.

Task

- If possible, watch the episode (Series 13, broadcast on 4 October 2022).
- Why do you think people complained?
- The restaurant critic Tejal Rao called the episode '*casually racist*' (Rao, 2022). What do you think she meant by this?

What is sometimes referred to as 'casual' or 'everyday' racism may not be overt or intentional, but it can still embolden or encourage prejudice. Through jokes and stereotypes, this type of racism becomes normalised and infused into daily life. Referring to 'the Mexicans' (or any other group, such as 'the deaf') assumes homogeneity and negates individual identities.

Teachers may understandably be keen to include students by referring to their identity, but care needs to be taken as identities are multifaceted, and one aspect of their identity does not necessarily define them.

Gender

In the 1970s, overt sexism was commonplace on TV. The *Carry On* films focused on women's body parts and innuendo; *On the Buses* featured a short-sighted female who was routinely the butt of sexist jokes; and *The Benny Hill Show* routinely had a sketch involving a milkman chasing young bikini-clad women. In TV car advertisements, it was not uncommon to have scantily clad young women draped across the bonnets, supposedly to promote sales. Times have changed, but this is not to suggest that more subtle and nuanced forms of sexism are not still evident in TV programmes today or that misogyny within the industry has disappeared.

The shift away from overt sexism on TV has not been matched by more gender-neutral curriculum and job choices. In the main, students in FE continue to choose subjects aligned to stereotypical, traditional male and female gender identities. It is difficult to pinpoint one main causal variable for gendered differences in subject choice. Sociologists agree that the reasons are complex and due to a multitude of factors. Socialisation, peer pressure and role models (or lack of role models) all play their part. Gender stereotyping views held by parents and teachers may affect the self-concepts of young people which, in turn, are reinforced by their peers and by the media.

Whether it is apprenticeships, T levels or BTEC courses, females dominate in health and social care and education and males in construction (Thompson, 2023). There have been many initiatives over a long period to encourage females into male-dominated course choices and vice versa, evidently with limited success. There may be a paradox of choice. By providing choices, FE might be reinforcing gender stereotypes, as students tend to enrol on courses where they feel most comfortable.

Task

- To what extent are skills-based courses gendered in your institution?
- Investigate what has been done, if anything, in your institution in recent years to encourage potential students to make less traditional choices.

Sexuality

Until recently, *Strictly Come Dancing* and *Dancing on Ice* had consistently represented partner dancing as a pairing between a male and a female. Heterosexuality and conventional gender roles are deeply entrenched in ballroom dancing and figure skating (Harman, 2019). Male dancers lead, invite the female to dance, support her, set the pace and navigate them both around the dancefloor or rink.

In 2020, same-sex pairings were introduced for the first time, initially with two females in *Strictly Come Dancing*, and then the following year with male/male partnerships in both shows.

Research by Wong et al (2021) is cautious about the positive impact of this on the viewing public but suggests that the media framed their reporting of these programmes as evidence of a progressive British society, generally supportive of same-sex dance couples and LGBTQ+ visibility. In turn, viewers who submitted complaints were positioned as a homophobic minority. After a performance, one of the *Strictly Come Dancing* male/male pairings, John Whaite, said, '*if we'd had this on TV when we were younger, life would have been a completely different place*' (Harrison, 2021).

Social class

A sub-genre of reality TV, known as 'structured reality', purports to portray ordinary people going about their lives. It presents this in the format of a conventional drama, blurring the traditional lines between documentary and soap. Two examples of this blend of fact and drama are *Made in Chelsea*, about rich young adults in West London, and *The Only Way Is Essex*, featuring a cast of real people who conform to the stereotypes of Essex man and Essex woman. Superficially these may reflect class differences, but in effect these programmes are heavily edited. It could be argued that they say more about the views of producers who present stereotypes that align to what they think viewers expect from certain types of people.

Pierre Bourdieu, a well-known sociologist, argued that middle-class or wealthier families transmit knowledge, behaviour, attitudes and cultural experiences to their children, who in turn convert this cultural capital into their own educational success (Bourdieu, 1986).

Research for the Sutton Trust by Lisauskaite et al (2021) confirms that young people from a more disadvantaged background, as indicated by eligibility for free school meals (FSM), are more likely to study in the FE sector rather than take the traditional academic route of A levels at school and then higher education (HE). The same research indicates that within FE colleges young people eligible for FSM are more likely to be studying for lower-level qualifications at level 1 or below, relative to the non-FSM group. However, taking account of prior attainment, a young person who attended an FE college and was eligible for FSM is as likely to reach HE as their FE college peers who were not entitled to FSM. This suggests that the FE sector is playing some role in social mobility, given the higher likelihood that young people from less advantaged backgrounds attend FE colleges in the first place.

Task

- To what extent, if at all, do you agree with the following view?

    ... all representations are at some level always about class. Television in particular, with its stories of everyday life and 'ordinary people', represents the structures of social relationships, from the most intimate to the most global, which are always about class.

    (Skeggs and Wood, 2011, p 15)

Age

Research reveals that media depictions of ageing and older people are largely negative (Royal Society for Public Health, 2022). Portrayals on TV, and in the media generally, reinforce stereotypes and assumptions, and it is suggested that this may lead to ageism and age discrimination. A key finding of a project reviewing societal age stereotypes in the media found that negative descriptions of older adults outnumber positive ones by six times (R Ng 2021). This research covered both the UK and USA as these have the largest media organisations and therefore significant power to shape public opinion. Negative descriptions of older people tend to be physical, while positive ones are more likely to be behavioural.

Age stereotypes often reflect oversimplified generalisations about how older people ought to behave. There are exceptions, of course, and some reality TV shows are at the forefront of demonstrating that age need not be a barrier to learning new skills or keeping fit and strong. For example, six of the 15 *Strictly Come Dancing* contestants in 2023 were aged 50 plus, one of whom, Angela Rippon, turned 79 years old during the series.

The FE sector, with around 2.7 million students aged 19 or over (Gov.UK, 2023), has a good track record in educating and (re)training adults. When discussing the practice of teaching adults, educators sometimes prefer the term *andragogy* to *pedagogy*. Andragogy is most widely associated with Malcolm Knowles. Knowles (1980) suggests that with pedagogy the student is dependent on the teacher, while andragogy assumes that adults are self-directing. This has an impact on how teachers teach, as with adult learners they can acknowledge and build upon their students' wealth of experience.

Task

- As an adult student on a teaching training programme, to what extent do (or did) tutors draw on *your* prior attainment and experience?
- If you teach both younger students and adults, do you adjust your teaching style? If so, how? Are adults more motivated, as Knowles asserts, and why do you think that might be? If you teach only one age group, discuss these questions with a colleague who teaches both younger and older students.

Intersectionality

The intersectionality of social class with other factors, such as gender and race, creates complex challenges, particularly for students with learning difficulties and/or disabilities. Students from lower social classes are more likely to face barriers in accessing necessary resources and support (Ainscow, 2012; Reay, 2012). Understanding these intersections is important in developing inclusive approaches to teaching and support (Tomlinson, 2012). In addition, the Covid-19 pandemic and the lockdown that followed in 2020 highlighted a digital divide. The groups least likely to have home internet access, just behind those aged over 65, are lower-income households and the most financially vulnerable (Ofcom, 2021a). Increasing levels of digital poverty widen the gap between students from different socio-economic classes. This can have a significant impact on students with LDD from lower social classes, limiting their opportunities to develop necessary digital skills (Selwyn, 2012).

Task

- If possible, investigate how your placement or teaching institution analyses student achievement, retention and attendance data. Are these analysed by age, gender, ethnicity and disability? If so, what patterns, if any, can be detected?
- Ask colleagues their views on the extent to which they think social class and/or a digital divide has an impact on the students they teach.

Language

Language is powerful. The language a teacher uses can help students to feel valued and included. Unfortunately, language can also offend, marginalise or misrepresent individuals and communities, and perpetuate stereotypes.

Language is at the heart of the 'culture war'. According to one study, a majority of 54 per cent in the UK feels that the country is divided by a culture war (Duffy et al, 2022). Central to this debate is the word 'woke'. African-American in origin, it entered the mainstream to describe being politically alert and vigilant. The Oxford Dictionary definition of 'woke' is *'aware of social and political issues, especially racism'*. The word has become increasingly weaponised in the media to refer to anything deemed to be too liberal or too progressive. The same study (Duffy et al, 2022) found that more people now see 'woke' as an insult (36 per cent) than a compliment (26 per cent).

What constitutes inclusive language is constantly evolving, and preferred terminology is not always universally agreed. Keeping up to date is important as some terms become outdated and new ones emerge. Fear of making a mistake or offending someone can make teachers nervous. One writer on the topic suggests:

> *I believe an imperfect attempt at using inclusive language is better than avoiding any attempt to eliminate potentially harmful language. It is important to bring a sense of humility to the process of using inclusive language, setting aside ego, and welcoming correction and improvement.*
>
> (Likis, 2021)

Task

- In Chapter 3, there is a task relating to Gordon Ramsay, the TV chef, who swears and yells at those working in kitchens. That task requires you to consider 'professionalism'. Now, think again about this behaviour in a training kitchen. In your view does his language make the learning environment more inclusive or less inclusive?

Inclusion, diversity and well-being **87**

Viewers in the UK are increasingly concerned by the use of racist and transphobic language on television but are more tolerant of swearing, according to a report into changing social attitudes (Ofcom, 2021b). In this research, there was a difference in attitudes between older and younger people as to how to handle repeats of old TV programmes that no longer fitted with current social attitudes. Some older interviewees felt that films featuring white people who painted their faces darker to resemble a black person, as in *Carry On* films, should still be repeated. They argued that 'blackface' was socially acceptable when the film was made. However, most younger viewers and black participants in the study felt that repeating such programmes perpetuates outdated racist views and so should not be shown again.

Through their language and their teaching resources, FE teachers can embrace, celebrate and respect differences.

Task

- Review a sample of the teaching resources you use. To what extent do they *promote* diversity? For example, do the choices you make about books, podcasts, handouts, posters, video clips or external visitors challenge stereotypes and reflect people from different backgrounds and genders or with disabilities?

Even when teachers create an inclusive environment, challenge negative stereotypes and set a good example as to how to treat people respectfully, difficult situations can arise, as in the scenario in the next task.

Task

- Imagine a situation where your students are working in pairs on a practical task. As you walk around, you hear one of the students (student x) reprimand the other using racist, homophobic or sexist language. The recipient of this comment (student y) says nothing and carries on with the task in hand. Other students do not necessarily hear this exchange.
- Do you:
  - ignore it and continue walking around the class?
  - ask student x to see you at the end of the lesson?
  - discuss the issue with both student x and student y there and then?
  - stop the whole group, tell them what has just happened, and remind them all about unacceptable behaviour/language?
- Explain your answer.

This is a hypothetical scenario, and how best to handle incidents like this depends on the context. However, doing nothing as a teacher in this type of situation is not an option. Ignoring or downplaying an event of this kind could constitute complicity. Interrupting students who are busily working on a task to make an announcement is rarely a good idea, as it disrupts the flow of a lesson. You might tell student x at the moment you pass by, or later, that the language used is unacceptable. In doing so, it is important to focus on the *language* and *behaviour*, not the person. It may also be appropriate to set aside some time at the beginning of the next lesson, or in a group tutorial, not to name and shame anyone, but to remind the group about institutional equality, diversity and behaviour policies and any agreed ground rules. As with any teaching and learning activity, the students are more likely to buy into the policies if their participation is active rather than passive, with an opportunity to ask questions, voice their views and engage in a meaningful discussion.

5.4 WELL-BEING

The assertion that people who sign up for reality TV programmes are more likely to be vulnerable than other people is unsubstantiated. Tragically, suicides of former contestants prompted a parliamentary inquiry into reality television in 2019. As a consequence of this, Ofcom announced that it would extend its duty of care beyond under-18s and other vulnerable people to anyone made vulnerable by their participation in any television genre. This applies during production and broadcast, and afterwards, particularly on social media. As noted by Damian Collins MP, who chaired the inquiry: '*It's not a special duty of care. It's bringing them on a par with other professionals*' (Royal Television Society, 2021).

Student well-being

Indeed, in FE, providers are responsible for the safeguarding of all their students. Safeguarding extends beyond the physical environment to include the safety and well-being of students in both their physical and their mental health. It is the process of creating an environment for all students and staff that actively prevents harm, harassment, bullying, abuse and neglect.

The Association of Colleges' *Mental Health Survey Report* (2023a) indicates that '*colleges, across all age ranges, are dealing with increasing numbers of students experiencing mental health and wellbeing difficulties*'. While the report paints a very disturbing picture, it also highlights how the sector is responding to the challenges, citing increases in counselling support, better mental health training for staff and effective working with partner organisations to secure further funding and resources.

Many providers (208 colleges, as of June 2023) have signed up to the Association of College's Mental Health Charter. The charter encourages colleges to commit to:

- *Ensure that wellbeing and mental health work is led by a senior manager supported by a member of staff with particular responsibility for mental health.*

- *Have a wellbeing and mental health policy accompanied by a clear implementation action plan which is monitored regularly and reviewed annually.*

- Create an open and inclusive college ethos which includes respect for those with mental ill health.
- Promote equality of opportunity and challenge mental health stigma through curriculum teaching and also promote wellbeing through tutorial programmes.
- Provide appropriate mental health training for staff.
- Encourage and collect student views on mental health and wellbeing by working with the Students' Union and other student representative bodies.
- Ensure a consistent and positive approach to staff wellbeing.
- Provide targeted individual mental health support where appropriate or alternatively signpost to external support services.
- Provide relevant information to parents and carers.
- Establish effective links with local health and voluntary sector mental health groups.
- Promote the benefit that physical activity and sport has on mental wellbeing.

(Association of Colleges, 2023b, p 11)

As noted in Chapter 3, when teaching or conducting one-to-one tutorials, teachers need to be aware of boundaries and limits to their expertise. If they have concerns about a student's well-being, they should direct this student to specific support or seek advice from an appropriate colleague. Concerns might, for example, include health disorders, such as anxiety, depression, eating disorders or self-harming; drug or alcohol use; physical or emotional abuse, including bullying; and financial or housing situations, such as homelessness.

Task

- Familiarise yourself with the safeguarding policy of your work or placement institution. This will tell you what to do, or who to speak to, if you have safeguarding concerns about a student.
- Find out who is the designated safeguarding lead (DSL) at the institution. DSLs provide support to staff to carry out their safeguarding duties and liaise closely with other services such as local authority children's social care and the police.

In addition to promoting students' general well-being, FE providers are required to have due regard to preventing students from being drawn into terrorism. This is linked to encouraging students to respect other people with particular regard to the protected characteristics of the Equality Act 2010. These are the following:

- age;
- disability;
- gender reassignment;

- marriage and civil partnership;
- pregnancy and maternity;
- race;
- religion or belief;
- sex;
- sexual orientation.

Inclusive teaching, as described earlier, is important in this respect, in creating an ethos that embraces and celebrates difference. FE teachers are also required to help students to engage with the key values associated with being a citizen in a modern and diverse society. These values include democracy, the rule of law, individual liberty and mutual respect for different faiths and beliefs, as well as for those without faith. Depending on the context and institutional policy, these values might be discussed in discrete sessions or tutorials, or through extra-curricular activities, or they may be embedded in the curriculum.

Developing students' critical thinking skills can build their resilience to different types of extremist narratives. The importance of developing students' critical thinking skills is emphasised throughout this book. Hooks (2010, p 10) notes that this is not easy to do *'as most students resist the critical thinking process; they are more comfortable with learning that allows them to remain passive'*. She goes on to suggest that teachers who work diligently to teach critical thinking often become discouraged when their students resist. It is important to persevere, as it is worth the effort. Whatever the subject, teachers can provide students with opportunities to weigh evidence, debate and make reasoned arguments. As well as learning how to argue and defend points of view, students should also learn how to recognise misinformation and 'fake' news, particularly online.

Role reversal is role play where students argue for a viewpoint they do not actually agree with. A carefully prepared and planned role reversal activity with a group of students can be very productive in helping them to understand each other's perspectives and to promote greater empathy. Teachers can make a professional judgement as to whether it is best to undertake this activity in pairs or to have one pair debate in front of the rest of the group. With the latter scenario, observers may vote for or against the argument, both before and after the debate, to see if anyone has been persuaded to change their viewpoint.

Task

- Review a course you teach and reflect on how you might embed these values: democracy, the rule of law, individual liberty and mutual respect for different faiths and beliefs.
- Think about how you might incorporate a role reversal activity into your teaching.

- Devise an activity to help students to understand the nuances associated with misinformation, at the same time developing their research, digital literacy and critical thinking skills. For example, business studies, hair and beauty, computing or construction students might investigate relevant industries or companies to understand the extent to which they may be 'greenwashing', that is, presenting misleading information and unsubstantiated claims to deceive consumers into thinking their products are more environmentally friendly than they actually are.

Staff well-being

Well-being is important not just for students. It is critical for staff too. Teaching in FE is rewarding but it can be very demanding and stressful, particularly for those new to the role. Teachers need to develop resilience to cope with the increased requirements to respond to the support needs of their students.

Without taking care of yourself, you will not have the energy to help your students. There is no shortage of generic advice and guidance on self-care, much of which is similar to the following list, which is taken from the National Institute of Mental Health.

- **Get regular exercise.** *Just 30 minutes of walking every day can help boost your mood and improve your health. Small amounts of exercise add up, so don't be discouraged if you can't do 30 minutes at one time.*
- **Eat healthy, regular meals and stay hydrated.** *A balanced diet and plenty of water can improve your energy and focus throughout the day. Also, limit caffeinated beverages such as soft drinks or coffee.*
- **Make sleep a priority.** *Stick to a schedule, and make sure you're getting enough sleep. Blue light from devices and screens can make it harder to fall asleep, so reduce blue light exposure from your phone or computer before bedtime.*
- **Try a relaxing activity.** *Explore relaxation or wellness programs or apps, which may incorporate meditation, muscle relaxation, or breathing exercises. Schedule regular times for these and other healthy activities you enjoy such as journaling.*
- **Set goals and priorities.** *Decide what must get done now and what can wait. Learn to say 'no' to new tasks if you start to feel like you're taking on too much. Try to be mindful of what you have accomplished at the end of the day, not what you have been unable to do.*
- **Practice gratitude.** *Remind yourself daily of things you are grateful for. Be specific. Write them down at night or replay them in your mind.*
- **Focus on positivity.** *Identify and challenge your negative and unhelpful thoughts.*
- **Stay connected.** *Reach out to your friends or family members who can provide emotional support and practical help.*

(National Institute of Mental Health, 2024)

As a teacher in FE, to reduce stress it can be helpful to:

- be willing to ask for help, ideas and advice from colleagues;
- plan your teaching so that, during your lessons, it is the students who are working hard rather than you;
- use and adjust existing teaching resources rather than always starting from scratch in designing your own;
- minimise time spent marking at home in the evenings. Mark students' work, if possible, during lessons while students are working on a task and encourage peer assessment so that students can mark each other's work;
- reflect on your practice. This may appear to be counter-intuitive if you are feeling overwhelmed, as it might seem like another task, creating more stress. However, taking the time to reflect on and analyse your teaching practice helps you to identify what works and what does not work with different groups of students. It gives you a better understanding of your strengths and weaknesses. This information enables you to adjust aspects of your practice and to become a more confident and expert teacher.

Task

- Find out who to contact in your work or placement organisation should you need support.
- List the ways in which you are prioritising your own well-being, reflecting on your work/life balance.

5.5 CONCLUSION

All students in FE should feel safe, secure and respected. Managers and governors in educational institutions have a responsibility to create an appropriate culture, through policies, guidance, role modelling and staff training. It is teachers, though, who have the most direct contact with students and who, through promoting inclusion, diversity and well-being, play a key role in providing an environment in which all students can flourish.

REFERENCES

Ainscow, M (2012) Moving Knowledge Around: Strategies for Fostering Equity within Educational Systems. *Journal of Educational Change*, 13: 289–310.

Association of Colleges (2023a) *AoC Mental Health Survey Report*. [online] Available at: https://feweek.co.uk/wp-content/uploads/2023/03/AoC-Mental-Health-Survey-Report-2023.pdf (accessed 11 February 2024).

Association of Colleges (2023b) Mental Health Charter. [online] Available at: https://www.aoc.co.uk/corporate-services/mental-health-wellbeing-2/aoc-mental-health-charter-framework-2 (accessed 11 February 2024).

Birkbeck, University of London (nd) About Us. [online] Available at: www.bbk.ac.uk/research/centres/neurodiversity-at-work/about-us (accessed 11 February 2024).

Bourdieu, P (1986) The Forms of Capital. In Richardso, J G (ed) *Handbook of Theory and Research in the Sociology of Education* (pp 241–58). New York: Greenwood Press.

Disability Horizons (2020) Briony May Williams: Bake Off Semi-finalist and TV Presenter Who Lives with a 'Little Hand'. [online] Available at: https://disabilityhorizons.com/2020/07/briony-may-williams-bake-off-semi-finalist-and-tv-presenter-who-lives-with-a-little-hand (accessed 11 February 2024).

Duffy, B, Stoneman, P, Hewlett, K, May, G, Woollen, C, Norman, C, Skinner, G and Gottfried, G (2022) *Woke, Cancel Culture and White Privilege – the Shifting Terms of the UK's 'Culture War'*. London: King's College London, The Policy Institute and Ipsos. [online] Available at: www.kcl.ac.uk/policy-institute/assets/the-shifting-terms-of-the-uks-culture-war.pdf (accessed 11 February 2024).

Equality Act 2010 [online] Available at: www.legislation.gov.uk/ukpga/2010/15/contents (accessed 11 February 2024).

Faragher, J (2023) Thinking Differently. *InTuition*, Summer: 15–17.

Gov.UK (2023) Further Education and Skills. [online] Available at: https://explore-education-statistics.service.gov.uk/find-statistics/further-education-and-skills (accessed 11 February 2024).

Harman, V (2019) *The Sexual Politics of Ballroom Dancing*. Palgrave.

Harrison, E (2021) Strictly Come Dancing Viewers Moved to Tears over John and Johannes's Support Messages. *The Independent*, 11 December. [online] Available at: www.independent.co.uk/arts-entertainment/tv/news/strictly-come-dancing-john-johannes-gay-b1974358.html (accessed 11 February 2024).

Hooks, B (2010) *Teaching Critical Thinking: Practical Wisdom*. New York; London: Routledge.

Hoole, G (2023) Addressing Social Class Disparities in SEND Support and Development. FE News, 19 June. [online] Available at: www.fenews.co.uk/exclusive/addressing-social-class-disparities-in-send-support-and-development (accessed 11 February 2024).

Knowles, M S (1980) *The Modern Practice of Adult Education: From Pedagogy to Andragogy*. New York: Cambridge, The Adult Education Company.

Likis, F (2021) Inclusive Language Promotes Equity: The Power of Words. *Journal of Midwifery & Women's Health*, 66(1): 7–9.

Lisauskaite, E, McIntosh, S, Speckesser, S and Espinoza, H (2021) *Going Further: Further Education, Disadvantage and Social Mobility*. London: Sutton Trust.

Long, N (2017) Friday Talks to Bake-off Queen Nadiya Hussain. Gulf News, 24 March. [online] Available at: https://gulfnews.com/friday/art-people/friday-talks-to-bake-off-queen-nadiya-hussain-1.1997115 (accessed 11 February 2024).

National Institute of Mental Health (2024) Caring for Your Mental Health. [online] Available at: www.nimh.nih.gov/health/topics/caring-for-your-mental-health (accessed 11 February 2024).

Ng, K (2021) Inspired by Strictly's Rose? Here's How You Can Start Learning Sign Language. *The Independent*, 17 December. [online] Available at: www.independent.co.uk/life-style/strictly-rose-ayling-ellis-sign-language-b1978075.html (accessed 11 February 2024).

Ng, R (2021) Societal Age Stereotypes in the U.S. and U.K. from a Media Database of 1.1 Billion Words. *International Journal of Environmental Research and Public Health*, 18(16): 8882. [online] Available at: www.ncbi.nlm.nih.gov/pmc/articles/PMC8391425 (accessed 11 February 2024).

Ofcom (2021a) Digital Divide Narrowed by Pandemic, but Around 1.5m Homes Remain Offline. [online] Available at: www.ofcom.org.uk/news-centre/2021/digital-divide-narrowed-but-around-1.5m-homes-offline (accessed 11 February 2024).

Ofcom (2021b) *Public Attitudes towards Offensive Language on TV and Radio*. Ipsos MORI research for Ofcom. [online] Available at: www.ipsos.com/en-uk/public-attitudes-towards-offensive-language-tv-and-radio (accessed 11 February 2024).

Rao, T (2022) 'Mexican Week' Was Not an Accident for 'The Great British Baking Show'. *The New York Times*, 14 October. [online] Available at: www.nytimes.com/2022/10/14/dining/great-british-bake-off-mexican-week.html (accessed 11 February 2024).

Reay, D (2012) What Would a Socially Just Education System Look Like? Saving the Minnows from the Pike. *Journal of Education Policy*, 27(5): 587–99.

Royal Society for Public Health (2022) *That Age Old Question*. [online] Available at: www.rsph.org.uk/static/uploaded/a01e3aa7-9356-40bc-99c81b14dd904a41.pdf (accessed 11 February 2024).

Royal Television Society (2021) Ofcom's New Duty of Care Guidelines to Protect TV Talent. [online] Available at: https://rts.org.uk/article/ofcoms-new-duty-care-guidelines-protect-tv-talent (accessed 11 February 2024).

Selwyn, N (2012) Making Sense of Young People, Education and Digital Technology: The Role of Sociological Theory. *Oxford Review of Education*, 38(1): 81–96.

Skeggs, B and Wood, H (2011) *Reality Television and Class*. London: Palgrave Macmillan.

The Guardian (2023) Rose Ayling-Ellis: 'I Felt Free to Be Me'. 18 June. [online] Available at: www.theguardian.com/tv-and-radio/2023/jun/18/rose-ayling-ellis-i-felt-free-to-be-me (accessed 11 February 2024).

Thompson, K (2023) Gender and Subject Choice. [online] Available at: https://revisesociology.com/2023/02/13/gender-and-subject-choice (accessed 11 February 2024).

Tomlinson, S (2012) *A Sociology of Special Education*. Abingdon: Routledge.

Wong, Y N, Harman, V and Owen, C (2021) Analysing Media Reactions to Male/Male Dance Partnerships on British Reality TV Shows: Inclusive Masculinity in Strictly Come Dancing and Dancing on Ice. *International Journal of the Sociology of Leisure*, 4: 397–413.

Education for sustainable development

6.1 INTRODUCTION

This chapter starts by outlining in section 6.2 the role FE can play in bringing about change and achieving sustainability goals. In sections 6.3 and 6.4, it goes on to review the sustainable organisation and FE staff attitudes to, and practice in, educational sustainable development. In section 6.5 on the curriculum, different models and structures are outlined, noting issues around inclusivity, English and mathematics, industry placements and resources. The remaining sections focus on sustainability in jobs and skills (section 6.6); teaching and learning activities (section 6.7); TV programmes as teaching and learning resources (section 6.8); and planning for sustainability (section 6.9).

6.2 CONTEXT

The further education and training (FE) sector has a critical role to play in combatting climate change and achieving broader sustainability goals. It is uniquely placed to bring about transition and transformation in our society. FE is the pipeline for the workforce of many industries, employers and sectors which have a critical role to play in sustainable development, including construction, manufacturing, agriculture, catering and transport. The sector reaches millions of learners from all walks of life. It employs over 100,000 staff and reaches communities in every town and city in the country. Imagine if everyone in the FE community – staff, learners, partners – had the knowledge, skills, attributes and agency required to be part of creating a sustainable and just future.

(Education and Training Foundation, 2021, p 2)

By 2023 we will:

develop an occupational standard for further education teaching which explicitly requires all new teachers to integrate sustainability into their teaching, through modelling sustainable practices and promoting sustainable development principles in relation to their subject specialism.

(DfE, 2022a)

The occupational standard duly developed, which will have been met by all those completing the *Diploma in Teaching (Further Education and Skills)* or the related apprenticeship, is Duty 8:

Undertake relevant roles and duties and model sustainable practices, having regard to professional standards, demonstrating resilience and adaptability when dealing with challenge and change.

(Institute for Apprenticeships (IfATE), 2023)

Task

○ Watch an episode of *Our Planet* (Netflix) or *Planet Earth* (BBC iPlayer). What sustainability issues does the programme raise? Are these related to your subject(s) in any ways? Are there other sustainability issues that are closely related to your subject(s)?

Sustainability is a complex area and a useful way of understanding it is to consider the range of the United Nations' 17 Sustainable Development Goals (SDGs).

Goal 1: No Poverty

Goal 2: Zero Hunger

Goal 3: Good Health and Well-being

Goal 4: Quality Education

Goal 5: Gender Equality

Goal 6: Clean Water and Sanitation

Goal 7: Affordable and Clean Energy

Goal 8: Decent Work and Economic Growth

Goal 9: Industry, Innovation and Infrastructure

Goal 10: Reduce Inequalities

Goal 11: Sustainable Cities and Communities

Goal 12: Responsible Consumption and Production

Goal 13: Climate Action

Goal 14: Life Below Water

Goal 15: Life On Land

Goal 16: Peace, Justice and Strong Institutions

Goal 17: Partnerships for the Goals

(United Nations, nd)

6.3 THE SUSTAINABLE ORGANISATION

The Climate Action Roadmap for FE Colleges claims that in colleges in which sustainability has become established, the SDGs have become '*part of the conversation*' at the college, and that '*the college community are aware of the SDGs and students have a sense of how they might apply to their subject of study*' (Climate Commission for UK Higher and Further Education/Nous Group, 2020).

However, research by the Education and Training Foundation (ETF) paints a less rosy picture of institutions' embracing of sustainability as a whole:

Only 20% of respondents felt that their leadership team are driving positive changes which suggests support for FE leaders and governors is necessary to further enable organisations to contribute to sustainability goals. There was the same response rate (20%) for those who feel their organisation meets relevant legislation but does nothing beyond that. Others felt it was a reputation enhancing issue (19%) or an opportunity to save money (17%). Just 5% felt their organisation was undertaking research relevant to sustainability. Perhaps most notably, 24% of respondents didn't know what their organisational approach to sustainability was. This suggests that the sector and its providers need further support to communicate sustainability ambitions and activities, where these exist, to the workforce.

(Education and Training Foundation, 2021, p 26)

Task

- How far do you think the above is true of the institution in which you teach? This may involve discussions with managers, teaching and other staff and students. Focuses for discussion could be the five sustainability areas the *Roadmap* identifies:
    1. leadership and governance;
    2. teaching, learning and research;
    3. estates and operations (campus buildings and activities in, from and to them);
    4. partnerships and engagement;
    5. data collection.

The *SORTED Guide to Sustainability in Further Education* (Alliance for Sustainability Leadership in Education, 2023a) has 162 resources which might inform the above discussions.

6.4 FURTHER EDUCATION STAFF ATTITUDES TO, AND PRACTICE IN, EDUCATION FOR SUSTAINABLE DEVELOPMENT

The ETF research explored staff attitudes to, and practice in, sustainability with the following queries.

1. How far have staff received adequate training to embed sustainability in their work and to educate learners about sustainability?
2. Does the FE and training sector have a valuable role to play in achieving education and sustainability goals?
3. Does the current UK post-16 system adequately educate learners on sustainability issues?
4. Should all UK learners be taught about sustainability issues?
5. How far are staff familiar with the UN's sustainability goals?
6. Are staff familiar with their organisation's approach to sustainability?
7. Do staff feel sustainability is an issue for all parts of the organisation?

Task

○ Use the previous questions as prompts for discussion with your colleagues. How far do their views reflect those of the ETF's research sample, set out in the infographic in Figure 6.1?

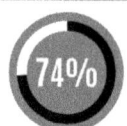 74% of teaching staff feel that they haven't received adequate training to embed sustainability in their work nor to educate learners about sustainability or climate change.

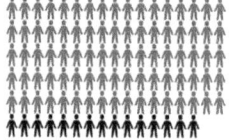 The majority of respondents (85%) agree that that the FE and Training sector has a valuable role to play in the achievement of sustainability goals.

68% feel that the current UK post-16 education system does not adequately educate learners on sustainability issues.  68%

Nearly all respondents (94%) believe that all UK learners should be taught about sustainability issues – this is often referred to as an ESD curriculum entitlement.

 43% of people are familiar with the sustainable development goals (SDGs).

61% of respondents (who teach a diverse range of subject specialisms) report that they already actively incorporate sustainability themes into their teaching/work to some extent.  61%

Only 35% of respondents agree that the curriculum requirements support delivery of sustainability issues.

24% of respondents didn't know what their organisational approach to sustainability is.   24%

 30% of respondents feel sustainability is an issue for all parts of their organisation.

Figure 6.1 Infographic: Teaching Staff Responses
Source: Education and Training Foundation, 2021

6.5 THE SUSTAINABLE CURRICULUM

Curriculum models

Curriculum models help teachers to put into practice certain educational principles and to map out the rationale for the use of particular teaching, learning and assessment approaches. Many authors and educationalists refer to two polarised curriculum models: the *product* model and the *process* model (Neary, 2003).

The product model (Tanner and Tanner, 2007; Walker and Soltis, 2009) focuses on the outcomes of learning, on what is to be learned when learning is completed. In this respect, it reflects a more behaviourist approach to learning, concerning itself with what students will be able to do at the end of a learning session. Applying an outcomes approach in mathematics, for example, would focus on whether the student had come to the correct sum, result or solution.

The process model (Bruner, 1992) is concerned with the 'how' of learning, the processes and procedures of learning, seeing the learner as active and learning mainly by doing. Applying a process approach in mathematics, for example, would focus not on whether students had come to the correct sum, result or solution but on how they had reached this in their working out.

In addition to the product and process models, other models include the *content* model and the *situational* model (Armitage et al, 2016). The content model (Reigeluth, 1999) focuses on the 'what' of learning, the knowledge and understanding learners will acquire. This traditional approach to education, focusing on the transmission of subject knowledge from subject experts to students, can trace its roots back to the medieval era. The trivium comprising logic, grammar and rhetoric established a basis on which the quadrivium of geometry, arithmetic, music and astronomy could be built.

The situational model (Lawton, 1983) focuses on the context or situation of learning. The curriculum of a music conservatoire would therefore be distinctive and related to the culture of music, whereas a brickwork curriculum in an FE college or workplace would reflect the world of construction. The learning of vocational skills, with which this book is primarily concerned, may seem, on the face of it, to conform to an outcomes or skills model but, as we saw in Chapters 2 and 3, knowledge, understanding, skills and abilities are all interlinked. In effect, specific curricula do not necessarily conform to any particular model and in practice most will comprise a blend of more than one.

Task

- The learning tasks in Table 6.1 are required as part of a sequence of learning which conforms to one or more of these curriculum models. Link the learning tasks to the curriculum models. If in a group, you may wish to discuss your answers.

Table 6.1 Task to link activities to curriculum model(s)

Learning task	Curriculum model(s)
1. In hairdressing, dyeing hair.	
2. As a bespoke tailor and cutter, understand the characteristics of a variety of fabrics.	
3. As a police officer, manage and conduct effective and efficient investigations.	
4. As a counsellor, listen empathically to a client.	
5. In horticulture, identify plant types.	
6. As a tiler, work out the number of tiles required for a specific area of floor.	
7. Lift a patient safely.	
8. As a domestic plumber, change a tap washer.	
9. As a musician, follow a musical score at the same time as following the conductor.	
10. As a chef, work quickly as well as effectively.	

Curriculum structures

Often within the FE sector, the term 'curriculum model' is used to determine the practicalities of how to structure teaching, learning and assessment within a given programme.

Some programmes, such as T levels, are structured around a *core* and *specialisms*. The core comprises a set of central, general foundation skills or knowledge relevant across the industry or sector, and common to all occupational specialisms. For example, students undertaking the T level Health route, having completed the core, choose a *specialism* offering entry to different health occupations. Depending on what the provider can offer, students might focus on adult nursing, midwifery, mental health, the care of children and young people, therapy teams or dental nursing.

The various components of any programme might relate to each other in different ways. Approaches might be the following.

- **Consecutive** – components are delivered in sequence.
- **Concurrent** – components are delivered simultaneously.
- **Combined** – components are combined throughout the programme.

Each approach has pros and cons, from an educational standpoint. For example, an advantage of the *consecutive* model is that it lends itself to a spiral curriculum (Bruner, 1960), in which the foundations are introduced and then revisited in later components, with deepening layers of complexity. It allows teachers to scaffold the development process (Vygotsky, Chapter 2) and students to apply, consolidate and extend their learning sequentially throughout the programme. The *concurrent* model might reinforce connections between different aspects of content and provide better opportunities to link theory and practice. It is likely that some of the modules of your teacher training programme are offered concurrently. The *combined* model may allow students to explore and apply different aspects of content in varying combinations (adapted from DfE, 2022b).

Whatever the model, in terms of assessment, as discussed in Chapter 4, consideration needs to be given to the validity, reliability, authenticity and practicality of any tasks. With a variety of components within a given model, there is also an opportunity to incorporate synoptic assessments. These require students to synthesise their learning from two or more modules within a programme. Students can demonstrate the breadth and depth of connections they have made between topics, and they may also be able to apply specific skills, knowledge and understanding taught in one part of the programme to other aspects of the course. If all students were required to undertake a mandatory module in sustainability, they could apply what they have learned in that module to their specialism.

Two key challenges for FE providers within any of the models are (a) English and mathematics and (b) industry placements. As highlighted in Chapter 3, with English and mathematics, debates centre around whether to embed the provision within vocational programmes or to offer discrete, specialist courses.

Task

- In Chapter 3 you were asked in one task to describe the model (embedded or discrete) for English and mathematics used in your workplace or placement provider. Revisit that task and think about the pros and cons of that model in supporting the students you teach.

Industry placements

Industry placements can be day-release, usually one day per week over one or two years (sometimes referred to as 'long and thin'); blocked, for example, every weekday for a nine-week period; or a mixture of day-release and blocked. Consideration needs to be taken of how best to align placements to the curriculum structure and to students' and employers' needs. The timing, structure and location of placements are significant for teachers. For example, a group of students on a digital production, design and development T level might return from a block placement working with a range of different employers, having all acquired very different technical skills. Teachers then need to plan lessons, taking into account each student's newly acquired experience, knowledge and skills.

Task

o In programmes like *The Voice*, *Dancing on Ice* and *Strictly Come Dancing*, contestants learn skills very intensely, practising each day, and they usually make rapid progress. In contrast, in *Big Dreams, Small Spaces*, Monty Don helps gardening enthusiasts to develop their gardening knowledge and skills by undertaking a project over a much longer period, as described in Chapter 3. If possible, watch clips from these programmes and with this in mind, think about the advantages and disadvantages of both day-release and block placements for (a) students, (b) employers and (c) teachers.

o Think about your own placement as a trainee teacher. Whether day-release, block or a mix of both, what are/were the pros and cons? If possible, share views with colleagues on the same programme.

Universal design for learning

Universal design for learning (UDL) is an educational framework that applies universal design principles to learning in order to accommodate the needs and abilities of *all* students. The aim is to eliminate at the design stage any potential hurdles. UDL stems from the social model of disability, as discussed in Chapter 5, which places the problem within the environment rather than with the individual who has the disability (Collins, 2014). The aim of UDL is to create a curriculum model, and associated resources and activities, that gives all students an equal opportunity to succeed and does not present any barriers. It is about building in flexibility so that all students benefit. Focusing on UDL at an early stage removes the need to make adjustments as an afterthought once teaching has started.

Task

o If you are following a course of initial teacher education such as the *Diploma in Teaching (Further Education and Skills)* or *PGCE Further Education and Skills* or the apprenticeship *Teaching Young People and Adults within all Parts of the Education and Training Sector*, try to describe your programme in terms of the models discussed in this chapter. Or answer the following.

o Describe the model/structure of a programme you teach. An effective way of approaching this task is to consult the programme specification. If possible, carry out this task in subject groups or in groups of those teaching allied subjects, for example: sociology, psychology and health and social care. Consider:

– the purpose of the qualification;

– the range of individual unit titles.

- Then select four or five units of learning. For each, look at:
  - the learning aims;
  - unit content;
  - assessment approach and assessment criteria.

Resources

FE providers need to be pragmatic. In practice, how the curriculum is structured depends not just on sound educational principles but also on available resources. Resources include rooms, specialist equipment and, in particular, the availability of teachers with the relevant expertise and of employers offering substantial placement opportunities for students.

Finance is important. Investment in skills, in FE, is critical for the economy and for students who deserve a high-quality education. There is evidence to suggest that increases in spending on sport in the UK led to the winning of more Olympic medals (De Menezes, 2016). Imagine if all FE students had access to anything like the resources and the intensive, high-quality, one-to-one teaching enjoyed by participants on *The Voice*, *Dancing on Ice* and *Strictly Come Dancing*. Funding in 2022–23 was around £6800 for the academic year for each 16–19-year-old student in FE. It is not possible to compare this with the money spent per contestant to learn to sing, skate and dance on these reality TV shows, as the information is not publicly available. A freedom of information request to the BBC was unsuccessful (What Do They Know, 2022). One can assume the difference is significant.

Task

- Review the previous task. With the model you described, investigate the extent to which there is, or was, any tension between the 'ideal' model and availability of resources. For example, were certain options/specialisms not available? Were there gaps during the day between sessions, purely due to room, specialist equipment or teacher availability?

Education for sustainable development content in vocational curricula

Research by the Education and Training Foundation (2022) showed that *'the biggest barrier educators faced in bringing ESD to their learning and teaching was sustainability issues not being in their curriculum specifications. We wanted to better understand this barrier and identify who, how and where ESD was being brought to the FE experience for learners'* (p 2). In order to do this, the ETF examined the learning content of qualifications, which '*includes critical global issues such as climate change, biodiversity, disaster risk reduction, and sustainable consumption and production*' (p 5). They considered whether '*physical and virtual learning environments ... inspire learners to act for sustainability and whether learners [are] empowered to transform themselves and the society they live in*' (p 5). The ETF also explored whether qualifications enabled:

> *the transition to greener economies and societies, equipping learners with skills for 'green jobs', motivating them to adopt sustainable lifestyles and empowering them to be 'global citizens' who engage and assume active roles, both locally and globally, to face and to resolve global challenges and ultimately to become proactive contributors to creating a more just, peaceful, tolerant, inclusive, secure and sustainable world.*
>
> (Education and Training Foundation, 2022, p 5)

Task

- In the same subject groups as for the previous tasks, return to your programme specifications. Looking across the unit content of your qualification, make a judgement about whether the content has broad education for sustainable development (ESD) coverage, partial coverage or no coverage.

In engineering, ESD content could include:

- human impacts on natural habitats, species and systems and how these can be sustained;
- renewable energy systems;
- lifecycle analysis;
- sustainability in supply chains and sourcing;
- environmental impact assessments, planning and relevant legislation;
- hazard management and climate change adaptation;
- sustainability kitemarks, accreditation schemes and standards;
- guest speakers from local engineering firms with a sustainability-related purpose and/or strong sustainability performance;
- site visits to local projects with strong sustainability features.

In health and social care, ESD content could include:

- global public health issues and health inequalities;
- links between environmental and personal well-being;
- sustainable healthcare systems;
- sustainable resource management;
- behavioural science and community engagement.

Task

- In the same groups, and particularly if the outcome of the previous task was that your qualification had no or partial coverage, consider ways in which you might enhance the ESD content in the teaching of your subject(s).

6.6 SUSTAINABILITY IN JOBS AND SKILLS

Heritage craft skills

The Repair Shop is a very popular programme and in 2023 won the Daytime TV Award at the National Television Awards (voted for by viewers). The attraction of the programme is that people bring in items which are of enormous sentimental value and, apart from observing experts use often traditional heritage craft skills, the audience witnesses the powerful emotional impact when owners see the lovingly repaired item.

In spite of their obvious popularity, attracting recruits into apprenticeships in which apprentices would learn such craft skills is proving problematic:

> *Organ-building and watchmaking – skills passed down since the 1500s and now deemed 'critically endangered' – have been available as apprenticeship standards for five years but have yet to enrol any recruits.*
>
> *Stained glass-making, traced back to the 7th century, has recently been declared 'endangered' by the charity Heritage Craft, which publishes an annual 'red list'. Its apprenticeship failed to attract any interest, a year after jumping the many hoops involved in getting approval from the Institute for Apprenticeships and Technical Education's (IfATE). Heritage Craft partly blames its demise on that of another craft, mouth-blown flat glass-making, deemed 'extinct' after the only company making it, English Antique Glass, was forced to leave its Birmingham home because of redevelopment. This had a 'knock-on effect' on stained glass restoration. Other apprenticeships designed to keep traditional skills alive but which have failed to attract any apprentices include clockmaker, assistant puppet-maker, bookbinder and blacksmith, all because of a lack of ability to procure a training provider, an end-point assessor or, in the case of bookbinder, both.*
>
> (FE Week, 2023)

Task

- Watch an edition of *The Repair Shop*. Could any of the skills used be described as heritage craft skills? Should we be encouraging people to train to use these skills or do you think that advantages in technology have largely made them redundant?

> **Task**
>
> The Repair Café movement has grown dramatically in this country and many others.
>
> www.repaircafe.org/en
>
> - Find out about this and other community recycling projects in your area (your institution may already be involved with these). How might the skills taught in your subject areas be of use in these community projects?

Green skills and 'fusion' skills

It is estimated that, in the future, as a result of sustainable development, there will need to be around 60 new occupations or occupational pathways, most of them '[*embracing*] *in an integrated way digitisation and productivity improvements*' (Hasting-Evans, 2022, p 5). In addition, a further 300 to 350 existing occupations will need to be enhanced to incorporate so-called 'green skills'.

Overall, there will be two million green jobs in the UK by 2030. Hasting-Evans (2022) provides the main estimates of the likely impacts on '*new and significantly revised jobs*' from the *Green Jobs Taskforce Report* that was published by the government in July 2021.

- The buildings retrofit sector would need 12,000 workers to be trained every year, and then ramp up annual recruitment by up to 30,000 workers between years 2025 and 2030.
- By 2050, the domestic market for smart systems and flexibility solutions would support around 10,000 jobs plus 14,000 export jobs.
- In 2021 there would be over 410,000 jobs in low carbon businesses and their supply chains.
- Electric vehicle gigafactories could create up to 78,000 new jobs (both direct and in the supply chain), with 24,500 in battery manufacturing, 43,500 in the battery supply chain, and around 10,000 in EV manufacturing.
- Offshore wind will employ around 70,000 workers by 2026 (40,000 direct jobs and 30,000 jobs in the supply chain).
- Electricity networks will have 260,000 new jobs by 2050 plus 140,000 replacements.
- Around 100,000 (about 50%) of the jobs in the UK offshore energy sector (including offshore wind, hydrogen, CCUS [carbon capture usage and storage] activities, oil and gas) in 2030 are projected to be filled by workers transferring from oil and gas to offshore renewable roles.
- The UK currently has 120,000 qualified gas engineers and by 2050 the heat network sector could create between 20,000–35,000 direct jobs.
- There will be a need for between 7,500–15,000 heat pump installers a year to be trained just within the next 7 years, resulting in around 60,000 workers needed.

Education for sustainable development **107**

- *Over 16,000 jobs could be developed in environmental development – improving woodland, peatlands and urban parks.*
- *Research suggests that the growth of circular economy sectors, such as repair, remanufacture, refill, and servitisation, could lead to the creation of between 54,000–102,000 jobs across all regions in the UK by 2030.*
- *50,000 workers in automotive manufacturing will need retraining or upskilling by 2025.*

(Hasting-Evans, 2022, p 19, citing estimates from Green Jobs Taskforce, 2021)

Task

- In your subject or allied subject groups, consider what new vocational roles/jobs might be created in the future.
- In existing roles in your vocational area, in which of the following elements will staff need occupational updating regarding sustainability?

    - *Use of different, changed or new materials.*
    - *Use of different, changed or new equipment.*
    - *Use of new or changed ways of doing things embedding the benefits of the new digital technologies.*
    - *Minimising waste and maximising the use of recycled materials.*
    - *Green awareness for each sector or sub-sector so that all the levels in the sector, which is the operational, supervisory, management and strategic management, understand their contribution to Net Zero and climate change.*

(Hasting-Evans, 2022, p 17)

In order to carry out work in new, green jobs or in existing updated jobs a range of green skills will be necessary. These would be skills deployed in specific vocational areas. Examples include:

- a structural erector being trained to build a large structure in resin and laminated timber as an alternative to traditional steel frame erection;
- a carpenter installing inside timber walls and floors as an alternative to installing floors on a traditional block internal wall;
- a roofer also installing solar panels on a house after, or in place of roof tiles;
- a concreter using non-cement (green) concrete to build the clean/green hydrogen fuel plant;
- a gas boiler installer with ability to install heat pumps;

- a rail worker utilising, recycling and upgrading switching gear instead of installing completely new equipment;
- a process engineer using up to date technology and telemetry to reduce the power consumption on the engineering plant;
- a construction plant operative using demolished material instead of bringing in new stones and rocks;
- equipment suppliers training installers in how to use low power usage power tools; and
- drones being used for surveying, thus avoiding expensive and carbon emitting trips for teams of surveyors.

(Hasting-Evans, 2022, p 17)

Task

- In your subject groups, return to your awarding body subject specifications. Looking at specific units, identify what you believe are the key green skills that successful completion of these units will require. You might look at a combination of the unit content, the recommended assessment approaches for this content and assessment criteria.

Some organisations have identified a number of skills they have called 'fusion skills', skills arising out of the fusion or integration of a number of areas:

Fusion skills combine education, arts, design, technology and business, reflecting how life is transformed by the fusion of these disciplines, generating opportunities for new learning, businesses, products and services.

(Alliance for Sustainability Leadership in Education, 2023b, p 11)

The following 12 skills were identified to be fundamental to the future world of work.

1. Oral communication/presentation skills
2. Collaboration and teamwork
3. Initiative
4. Problem-solving
5. Organisational skills (planning, time management, prioritisation, multi-tasking)
6. Adaptability/flexibility
7. Written communication
8. Independent working/autonomy
9. Critical thinking
10. Resilience

11. Creativity

12. Analysis and evaluation skills

(Alliance for Sustainability Leadership in Education, 2023b, p 12)

Task

- Looking at a course you teach, identify how and when these skills are being developed by students and, if at all, assessed. For example, are there specific tasks that require these skills? To what extent do these skills appear in learning outcomes and/or assessment criteria? Are placement mentors helping students to develop these skills?
- To what extent are *you* developing these skills in your practice as a (trainee) teacher?
- If appropriate, create a pyramid of the 12 fusion skills, representing the prioritisation teachers of your subject would give to these fusion skills in their courses (as shown in Figure 6.2).

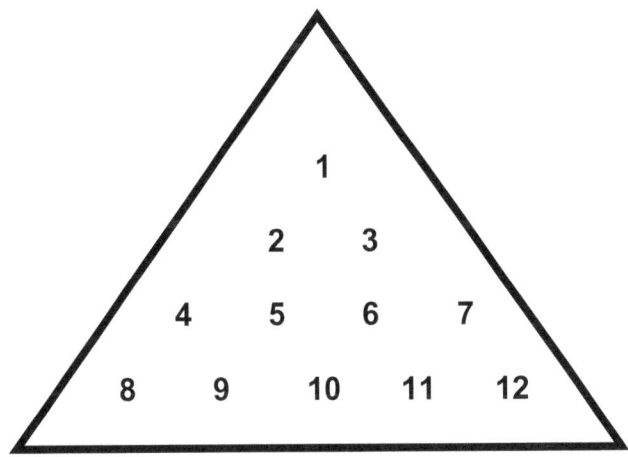

Figure 6.2 Pyramid of skills

6.7 TEACHING AND LEARNING ACTIVITIES FOR SUSTAINABILITY

In section 6.9, you will be asked to develop a scheme of work and lesson plans focusing on sustainability topic(s) in your subject area. Before tackling that task, it is helpful to think about any lesson in your subject where you might include a short session, or what we might call a 'vignette', which connects with a sustainability issue. The following are examples.

- A **business studies** tutor, during a session on stocks and shares, asks students to conduct a piece of research on green investment.
- A **hairdressing** tutor, in what is otherwise a practical lesson, shows a PowerPoint about sustainability relating to the craft. This might touch on:
  - the effect of discarded plastics entering the food cycle;
  - tightly woven mats made out of human hair which can be used in parks, around drains and in smaller waterways to treat minor pollution problems and oil spills;
  - salon sustainability – safe disposal of chemicals; excessive use of water.
- A **health and social care** tutor creates a global health map with students.
- An **animal care** teacher conducts a discussion about animal welfare and habitat conservation after students watch a YouTube video.
- A **catering** teacher shares research on the effect of food production on the environment.
- A **construction** tutor gives students a quiz regarding sustainable and non-sustainable construction materials.
- **Plumbing and heating** students are tasked with carrying out a cost–benefit analysis of the installation of heat pumps.
- **Travel and tourism** students consider the current efforts of a specific city or country (Venice, The Maldives) to manage eco-tourism issues.
- **Psychology** students are asked to pool ideas about how to motivate individuals to recycle.
- **Sports studies** students calculate the carbon footprint of a global sports event.

Task

- Consider lessons you have recently taught or those you are preparing for. Can you think of any appropriate vignettes you might include in these lessons?

6.8 TV PROGRAMMES AS TEACHING AND LEARNING RESOURCES FOR SUSTAINABILITY

There is now a wide and increasing range of TV programmes which involve or promote sustainability.

Waste Not (National Geographic): a series which deals with the global issue of waste management and disposal and looks at solutions to re-use, reduce and recycle waste.

Our Planet (Netflix): featuring the beauty and variety of animal life, the series shows how climate change can affect all living creatures and their habitats.

Bill Nye Saves the World (Netflix): the scientist invites experts and famous guests to his lab to explore subjects of scientific interest, many relating to sustainability.

Planet Earth (BBC): David Attenborough celebrates the wonders of our planet, highlighting environmental issues.

Blue Planet II (BBC): this series focuses on marine life and the effect on it of pollution, overfishing and climate change.

Cooked (Netflix): food writer Michael Pollan explores how cooking transforms our world and shapes food.

The Story of Stuff (YouTube): Annie Leonard's series explains the lifecycle of consumer goods and the effects of over consumption on the environment.

Cowspiracy: The Sustainability Secret (YouTube/Google Play Movies and TV/Apple TV) '*is a feature-length environmental documentary following film-maker Kip Anderson as he uncovers what he describes as the most destructive industry facing the planet today*'.

Years of Living Dangerously (Showtime/National Geographic): '*The weekly episodes feature celebrity hosts with a history of environmental activism and well-known journalists with a background in environmental reportage*'.

The Age of Consequences (Apple TV) investigates the links between climate change, resource scarcity and conflict, and examines how these factors can contribute to political instability and social unrest.

Task

o   Using one of the above programmes as a stimulus, or selecting one of your own choosing, create a learning activity (or activities) which could be part of a lesson you have taught or intend to teach.

6.9 PLANNING FOR SUSTAINABILITY

All teachers in FE will normally use a scheme of work (SOW) as the major planning tool to manage their teaching and their students' learning. The format of the SOW will depend on the institution, the subject and the nature of the units of learning making up the course/programme. A SOW will also be a guide for any substitute teacher or other subject colleague teaching on the programme. Although awarding body specifications will often prescribe the content and assessment approaches to units, individual teachers have considerable freedom in turning those specifications into living, breathing programmes of learning. Creating a SOW involves consideration of the following issues.

Sequence/structure

What will be the chronological sequence of the lessons/sessions? Reflecting on Chapter 2, are there key threshold concepts or skills which need to be addressed early in the SOW before students can move on to more complex concepts and skills? Are there knowledge, concepts and skills which need to be returned to and addressed throughout the lessons (what we call the 'spiral curriculum')? Do the lessons move from simple ideas and concepts to more complex ones? Or do lessons articulate – the end of one lesson dovetailing with the beginning of another (rather like TV serial episodes)?

Overview

There will be certain features of the sequence of learning which need to be clarified at the beginning. Does the SOW cover a course completely or a unit of learning within the course (more usual)? What are the guided learning hours (GLH) for the unit? Is there a finite number of lessons? How many? This gives the reader a useful gauge of the scale of the SOW.

Individual lessons/sessions

Go back to Chapter 3 and look at sections about aims and objectives, lesson content, teaching and learning activities. Do these involve individual, pair or group work and what are their timings, with teacher input and student input specified? Are there links to other sessions? How is this done? Through a plenary – when, at the beginning, halfway through, at the end? What resources will be used in the lesson and via which media? How will learning in the session be assessed (Chapter 4)? What differentiation will there be, if any, of content or assessment? How will lessons be evaluated, by whom and when? How inclusive are the resources? To what extent do they promote diversity?

Task

- Either alone or preferably with colleagues from the same or related subjects, develop a scheme of work. This should either be about a sustainable topic in your subject area or, if not, show how aspects of sustainability feature in your SOW in your aims and objectives, lesson content, teaching and learning activities, resources and assessment.

In the *Ultimate Wedding Planner* (BBC iPlayer) participants, in teams, are given the brief of planning a couple's wedding and a budget of £10,000. Each team member has a specialist set of skills – there is a florist, a DJ, a dancer, for example. Three judges monitor the planning and the event itself and, at the end, come to a judgement about how well both teams and individuals fared. Like *The Apprentice*, there is a paradox at the heart of the show: although participants are competing with one another, they are judged as individuals on how well they collaborate with each other. There is the usual elimination of a participant at the end of each show.

Task

- If possible, watch an episode(s) of the *Ultimate Wedding Planner.* There are six episodes in Series 1.
- Consider the parallels with your planning and teaching a lesson.

In the *Ultimate Wedding Planner*, at the start of the session, the judges make their assessment criteria clear: they want to see creativity, sensitivity to the couple's brief, precise (military) planning and an ability to manage the budget and come in under this as far as possible. One participant bemoans most weddings he has been to as '*copy and paste, copy and paste*' suggesting that many wedding planners lack imagination and creativity. The couples, at the beginning of the planning process, have only the bare bones of an idea – maybe a choice of wedding venue.

Teams are responsible for *design*, on the one hand – perhaps a central thematic idea, the décor, venue layout to go along with it. In Episode 1, the bride wants a '*floral wonderland*' so flowers become a major part of the design (and budget). On the other hand, a team is responsible for the *experience* or the nature of the event itself, the guests' journey, and the judges stress the importance of '*attention to detail*' in this journey. There is a head planner, tasked with co-ordinating each of the team's efforts and managing the budget. One of the experience team has the idea of creating a to-do list of items they will need for the day. There is pressure for these items to be sustainably resourced, if only to keep costs down ('*all we can do is the best with what we've got*', says the head planner, which might be a useful sentiment for a teacher with limited resources). Halfway, there is a judges' walk-through in which they will '*sense check decisions*', appraising the efficacy of team planning.

In Episode 1 the judges agree that there are '*far too many questions*' they have about what they have seen of planning thus far. On the wedding day itself, we see how well or not planners improvise when things go wrong. One judge thinks that a fatal error not rectified is like missing a train and even though you can run from station to station, you can never then catch the train. The planners have the idea of constructing 'truth booths' at the venue, where the couple and their guests record their own appraisals of the wedding day. (How do you use your students' views as a part of your evaluation of lessons? A truth booth in your classroom?)

Task

- Select one lesson from your SOW and plan it as if it were an event such as a wedding. Specify any sustainable resources you would use.

6.10 CONCLUSION

At the time of writing, not a day goes by without a key green issue hitting the headlines, whether that be sourcing energy, environmental pollution, sustainable transport, CO_2 emissions, famine and food production, or climate change. Many of these issues are refracted through the TV programmes we and our students watch regularly. These issues are having a major impact on all our lives currently and will continue to affect all of us in the future, particularly in teaching and learning in our FE institutions. Before leaving this chapter, consider again how sustainability is impacting on the key issues of the previous five chapters: the FE system as a whole, learning, teaching, assessment and inclusion.

REFERENCES

Alliance for Sustainability Leadership in Education (2023a) *SORTED Guide to Sustainability in Further Education*. [online] Available at: www.sustainabilityexchange.ac.uk/sorted_guide_to_sustainability_in_further_educa (accessed 11 February 2024).

Alliance for Sustainability Leadership in Education (2023b) *Fusion Skills: Education for Sustainable Development Toolkit*. [online] Available at: www.eauc.org.uk/fusion_skills_education_for_sustainable_develop (accessed 11 February 2024).

Armitage, A, Cogger, A, Evershed, J, Hayes, D, Lawes, S and Renwick, A (2016) *Teaching in Post-14 Education and Training*. 5th ed. Maidenhead: McGraw-Hill Education/Open University Press.

Bruner, J (1960) *The Process of Education*. Cambridge MA: The President and Fellows of Harvard College.

Bruner, J (1992) *Acts of Meaning*. Cambridge, MA: Harvard University Press.

Climate Commission for UK Higher and Further Education/Nous Group (2020) *The Climate Action Roadmap for FE Colleges*. Gloucester: Climate Commission for UK Higher and Further Education/Nous Group.

Collins, B (2014) Universal Design for Learning: What Occupational Therapy Can Contribute. *Occupational Therapy Now*, 16(5).

De Menezes, J (2016) Rio 2016: How Much Did Each Team GB Olympic Medal Actually Cost the UK Taxpayer?. [online] Available at: https://www.independent.co.uk/sport/olympics/rio-2016-team-gb-medals-how-much-did-each-cost-uk-tax-olympics-medal-table-a7203321.html (accessed 11 February 2023).

Department for Education (DfE) (2022a) *Sustainability and Climate Change: A Strategy for the Education and Children's Services Systems*. Policy paper. London: DfE. [online] Available at: https://www.gov.uk/government/publications/sustainability-and-climate-change-strategy/sustainability-and-climate-change-a-strategy-for-the-education-and-childrens-services-systems

Department for Education (DfE) (2022b) T Levels Support for Schools and Colleges: Action Plan for Considering Different Curriculum Models. [online] Available at: https://support.tlevels.gov.uk/hc/en-gb/articles/4406327202066-Action-plan-for-considering-different-curriculum-models (accessed 11 February 2024).

Education and Training Foundation (ETF) (2021) *Experiences of Education for Sustainable Development in the Further Education and Training Sector*. London: ETF.

Education and Training Foundation (ETF) (2022) *Leadership for ESD in the FE curriculum: A Review of Education for Sustainable Development (ESD) Approaches and Curriculum Content in Post-16 Qualifications in England*. London: ETF. [online] Available at: www.et-foundation.co.uk/wp-content/uploads/2021/11/Leadership-for-ESD-in-the-FE-curriculum-report.pdf (accessed 11 February 2024).

FE Week (2023) A Break with Tradition: The Crafts Fighting for Survival. [online] Available at: https://feweek.co.uk/a-break-with-tradition-the-crafts-fighting-for-survival (accessed 11 February 2024).

Green Jobs Taskforce (2021) *Green Jobs Taskforce: Report to Government Industry and the Skills Sector*. [online] Available at: www.gov.uk/government/publications/green-jobs-taskforce-report (accessed 11 February 2024).

Hasting-Evans, G (2022) *Greening the UK's Skills*. Sheffield: NOCN and British Association of Construction Heads. [online] Available at: www.nocn.org.uk/products/consultancy-and-research/greening-uk-skills (accessed 11 February 2024).

Institute for Apprenticeships (IfATE) (2023) *Learning and Skills Teacher*. [online] Available at: https://www.instituteforapprenticeships.org/apprenticeship-standards/learning-and-skills-teacher-v1-2 (accessed 11 February 2024).

Lawton, D (1983) *Curriculum Studies and Educational Planning*. London: Hodder and Stoughton.

Neary, M (2003) Curriculum Concepts and Research. In *Curriculum Studies in Post-compulsory and Adult Education: A Teacher's and Student Teacher's Study Guide* (pp 60–5). Cheltenham: Nelson Thornes Ltd.

Reigeluth, C M (ed) (1999) *Instructional-design Theories and Models: A New Paradigm of Instructional Theory, Vol. 2*. Mahwah, NJ: Lawrence Erlbaum Associates.

Tanner, D and Tanner, L M (2007) *Curriculum Development: Theory into Practice*. 4th ed. Upper Saddle River, NJ; Columbus, OH: Pearson Merrill Prentice Hall.

United Nations (nd) Sustainable Development Goals. [online] Available at: https://sdgs.un.org/goals (accessed 11 February 2024).

Walker, D F and Soltis, J F (2009) *Curriculum and Aims*. 5th ed. London: Teachers College Press.

What Do They Know? (2022) Strictly Come Dancing Production Cost. [online] Available at: https://www.whatdotheyknow.com/request/strictly_come_dancing_production (accessed 11 February 2024).

7 Expertise, professional development and a spot, swot and plot

7.1 INTRODUCTION

Chapters 1–6 focused on key themes for those training to teach in the FE sector. This chapter is concerned with the first stages of your career and your subsequent continuous professional development. In section 7.2 standards, qualifications and duties are explained. The development of expertise is explored in section 7.3 with a discussion about the stages of skill acquisition and the qualities of expert teachers. In section 7.4 potential professional development activities are examined. There is an opportunity in section 7.5 to engage in reflection and planning, with a three-part 'spot, swot and plot' activity. In section 7.6 the next steps after initial teacher education are outlined, before the chapter, and the book, are concluded in section 7.7.

7.2 STANDARDS, QUALIFICATIONS AND DUTIES

In Chapters 1 and 3 we considered the role of the teacher, particularly the professionalism of FE teachers and their identity as dual professionals. From September 2024, trainees new to the sector will take the *Diploma in Teaching (Further Education and Skills)*. Trainees completing this qualification will need to have met the same standards as those completing the FE teaching apprenticeship *Teaching Young People and Adults within all Parts of the Education and Training Sector*, with reference to the following occupational duties.

Duty 1: Promote a passion for learning and set high expectations of all students and support their personal and skills development.

Duty 2: Maintain a focus on outcomes, for all students, so that they recognise the value of their learning and the future opportunities available to them.

Duty 3: Demonstrate, maintain and evidence excellent pedagogy, subject, curriculum and industry knowledge and practice.

Duty 4: Plan, deliver and evaluate effective evidence-informed teaching using assessment, relevant systems and safe use of technology to support learning.

Duty 5: Work in a manner that values diversity, and actively promote equality of opportunity and inclusion by responding to the needs of all students.

Duty 6: Model professional relationships with students, colleagues and stakeholders that support the highest quality education and training.

Duty 7: Work within professional boundaries and legal and ethical standards to set clear expectations for engaging in learning for all students.

Duty 8: Undertake relevant roles and duties and model sustainable practices, having regard to professional standards, demonstrating resilience and adaptability when dealing with challenge and change.

In Chapter 3 you were familiarised with the *Professional Standards for Teachers and Trainers* which were introduced in 2014 and updated in 2022. The relationship of these standards to the practice of new and established FE teachers is likely to change from 2024. Hitherto, most providers of FE initial teacher training embedded these standards in their programmes, so that all trainees successfully completing programmes have also been seen to have met the standards. However, from 2024, new teachers need to meet the requirements of the occupational duties above, with the Professional Standards becoming aspirational for qualified teachers undertaking continuous professional development and gaining professional experience. In fact, the occupational duties and the Professional Standards correspond closely, as set out in section 7.5.

According to the Education and Training Foundation:

> *The Professional Standards are aspirational statements – they promote opportunities to develop excellent teaching and learning. For both new and experienced teachers and trainers, the Standards can be used by individuals to reflect on their practice and guide decisions on what can be developed and improved. Teaching and training teams can use the Standards to self-assess their strengths and development needs, and to stimulate conversations on how best to support learners and raise standards across the curriculum. The Standards are also expected to promote new and innovative forms of knowledge-sharing so that good practice is disseminated across organisational boundaries.*
>
> (Education and Training Foundation, 2022, p 6)

7.3 DEVELOPING EXPERTISE

The stages of skill acquisition

When watching *Strictly Come Dancing*, even if they know very little about dancing, viewers can easily see the difference between the professional experts and the novice contestants as soon as they take to the dancefloor. The experts have had years to hone their skills, during which time they will have had tuition, support, feedback and lots of practice, and won many contests. The novices, on the other hand, take part having had very little if any experience. As the series progresses, the contestants make progress. Some leave the contest in the first few weeks, having demonstrated to the viewers, and to themselves, that they are no longer beginners and that they may now be competent dancers. Those that remain until the final stages usually demonstrate that they have become proficient dancers. Finalists do not become experts, given the short time frame of the competition. However, occasionally, in the final dance, it is hard to distinguish between the most successful contestants and the professional experts.

This differing level of skill acquisition is seen in other TV programmes too. In *The Great British Bake Off*, *MasterChef*, *The Great Pottery Throw Down*, and *The Great British Sewing Bee*, the contestants are amateurs, but they are usually well beyond the novice stage before they start the contest. They expect that participation in the contest will enable them to develop further their knowledge and skills and, for some, it is an opportunity to consider becoming an expert professional in their chosen specialism.

Competition for places in these programmes is fierce. It is evident that potential contestants prepare well and recognise the need for a significant amount of practice before even applying. For example, Irini Tzortzoglou, who won *MasterChef* in 2019 at the age of 60, explains in an interview that she decided to enter *MasterChef* out of a need to feel challenged. The article continues:

> *Tzortzoglou was a reasonably good cook, who loved entertaining and could put together a decent dinner party menu, but competing on the show demanded a whole new skill level. 'I didn't want to embarrass myself by leaving in round one, so I trained myself for a year,' she says. She put in time, effort and money (including buying gadgets and overhauling her kitchen at home in Cumbria). 'I went to Athens, I ate at Michelin-star restaurants,' she says. 'I wanted to see what was happening with Greek food today. I watched a little bit of Greek MasterChef to see what the young chefs were doing. And then I started practising.'*
>
> (Saner, 2022)

In contrast, those who take part in the celebrity versions of these programmes, such as *The Great Celebrity Bake Off* or *Celebrity MasterChef* are often genuine novices. Much of the entertainment stems from the fact that these celebrities, who are successful in other aspects of their lives, such as acting, sport or comedy, make mistakes. They are not afraid to embarrass themselves as they are already established in their own career and so it does not damage their reputation. For viewers, the fact that things go wrong adds to enjoyment of the programme.

As seen in these programmes, a novice in the kitchen can follow a recipe. They may not understand anything about the recipe, but they put their trust into instructions that come from a reliable source. The novice can follow each step of the recipe and then demonstrate their skills by producing the final dish without any understanding of the relationships between the ingredients or the reasoning behind the processes or the order of the steps. As novices become more experienced, they adjust recipes, experiment with different ingredients and might eventually create their own.

The expert potters who demonstrate their knowledge and skills on *The Great Pottery Throw Down* make the task look so easy. They do not worry about how to centre their clay on the wheel head so that its outer edges spin perfectly smoothly with no bumps or wobbles. They have developed enough intuition to create something beautiful without actively thinking about all of the disparate elements involved in the process.

Just like these dancers, chefs and potters, teachers progress through various stages in their career and become more skilful. In thinking about how they move from their initial training and early career through to becoming an expert, it is helpful to reflect on the work undertaken by Dreyfus and Dreyfus (1986). They studied the skill acquisition process of airline pilots, chess players, car drivers and adult learners of a second language and claim to have observed a common pattern in all cases, which they call *'the five stages of skill acquisition'* (Dreyfus and Dreyfus, 1986, p 24). These stages are:

1. novice;
2. advanced beginner;
3. competent;
4. proficient;
5. expert.

In the novice stage, a person follows rules and so, for example, if learning to drive a car, they do as they are told by their instructor and so they change gear at a given speed and keep a certain distance from the car ahead of them. As an advanced beginner they start to act on the basis of experience rather than just rules. At this stage the driver may change gear according to engine sounds.

A nurse tutor may ask advanced beginner students to undertake a series of checks on a newborn baby in a ventilator but only at the competent stage would the students know in what order to do these according to their importance. This type of competence develops after having considerable experience, so at this stage

> ... people learn, or are taught, to adopt a hierarchical procedure of decision making. By first choosing a plan to organize the situation, and by then examining only the small set of factors that are most important given the chosen plan, a person can both simplify and improve their performance.
> (Dreyfus and Dreyfus, 1986, p 24)

Proficiency is shown in individuals who use intuition in decision making and develop their own rules to formulate plans. A potter may intuitively add more water to the clay or decrease the speed of the pottery wheel, while a chef might adjust the seasoning or add an additional ingredient. A proficient driver may intuitively realise they are driving too fast on a rainy day as they approach a bend in the road. They then decide whether to apply the brakes, remove their foot from the accelerator or merely reduce pressure.

Expertise is characterised when performance happens unconsciously and automatically and no longer depends on explicit knowledge. At this final stage, an expert:

> ... generally knows what to do based on mature and practised understanding ... the expert driver becomes one with their car, and they experience themselves simply as driving, rather than as driving a car, just as, at other times, they certainly experience themselves as walking and not, as a small child might, as consciously and deliberately propelling their body forwards ... With expertise comes fluid performance. We seldom 'choose our words' or 'place our feet' – we simply talk and walk.
> (Dreyfus and Dreyfus, 1986, p 31)

Task

- Think about an activity you enjoy doing, such as photography, cooking, dancing, pilates, pottery or gardening. Which stage are you operating at – novice, advanced beginner, competent, proficient or expert?

- Ask your tutor, or an advanced practitioner, or the person responsible for continuing professional development (CPD) where you teach if they recognise the Dreyfus and Dreyfus skills acquisition model in terms of their own transition from new teacher to expert teacher.

- To what extent does the Dreyfus and Dreyfus model accurately describe your developing expertise as a teacher?

It would be surprising if you consider this model as an accurate account of your development at this stage of your career. This is because, as we saw in Chapter 3, teaching expertise is not just a matter of following rules but requires skills, subject and pedagogic content knowledge, as well as professional values and behaviours. The staged model is attractive because it suggests a dynamic linear process in which we become more expert as we become more experienced.

Experienced colleagues are likely to confirm that teacher development is a messy business which seldom proceeds in a linear manner. One day your classroom management with one group may be assured; the following day, with another group, you lose control and you are not sure why. After one session, you leave the classroom beaming: the lesson has been a success, the students were engaged and stimulated. The next session falls flat. The students are clearly not engaged; they go off task in group work as they do not understand what is required of them.

At any one time, a teacher's practice is likely to show a spiky profile, with some aspects of professional performance more advanced than others. The most effective way for a teacher to manage their development is through the kind of reflection we considered in Chapter 2. Here we looked at Kolb's experiential learning cycle but, as noted then, whichever model of reflection you use, it is likely that, as well as encouraging your students to reflect on their work and progress in this way, you will be doing the same in terms of reflecting on your own practice as a teacher, trainer or trainee.

An inability or unwillingness to reflect candidly on professional practice is likely to restrict progress. Hence, we present you with the opportunity to reflect in section 7.4. But first, what are the qualities of the expert teacher you aspire to be?

The expert teacher

As in other professions, it may well take years of experience, learning and quite a few mistakes to become an 'expert' teacher. Given the complexity of teaching, it is not surprising that there is no one definition of teaching expertise or one-size-fits-all template for a lesson. However, there is some consensus about the key characteristics and practices of expert teachers. It is generally recognised that high-quality teaching cannot be described simply in terms of isolated competencies or checklists and that instead one has to try to capture *'the essence of a good teacher'* (Korthagen, 2004, p 77). To try to understand this essence, we will look at research by Coe et al; Hattie; Anderson and Taner; and Harper.

In researching what makes great teaching, Coe et al (2014) define 'effective' teaching as *'that which leads to improved student achievement using outcomes that matter to their future success'* (p 2). They argue that good teaching involves a combination of six components manifested at different times, noting that the very best teachers are those who demonstrate all the features. The first is pedagogical content knowledge. This relates to teachers' deep knowledge of their subject and how to teach it, as explored in Chapter 3. The second is quality of instruction. How teachers scaffold knowledge, teach and assess are examined in Chapters 2, 3 and 4. The third, classroom climate, highlights the importance of relationships between teachers and students, and students with each other. This is reflected in discussions about communities of practice and socially situated learning in Chapter 2, in discussions about collaborative learning in Chapter 3 and also when examining inclusive teaching in Chapter 5. The fourth, classroom management, is addressed in Chapter 3, while the fifth and sixth, teacher beliefs and professional behaviours, feature throughout the book.

Task

- To what extent do you think student progress and outcomes should be the yardstick by which teacher quality is measured? Should other factors be taken into consideration? If so, what are they?

In many ways, the six components outlined above are similar to the findings of earlier research undertaken by Hattie (1999, 2003), who identifies five dimensions that set apart expert teachers. This research concludes that expert teachers can:

- identify the best ways to represent the subjects they teach;
- create an optimal climate for learning within the classroom;
- monitor learning and provide feedback;
- believe all students can succeed;
- influence a range of student outcomes, not just examination results.

In another extensive and systematic review of the research on expert teaching (Anderson and Taner, 2023), the key salient findings indicate that:

> ... with regard to professional practice, expert teachers reflect extensively and often critically on their practice, help their colleagues frequently, and are continuous learners throughout their careers. Concerning knowledge, we find that expert

> *teachers have well-developed pedagogical content knowledge and knowledge about their learners. In the domain of pedagogic practice, we observe that expert teachers display flexibility in the classroom, build strong interpersonal relationships with their learners, whom they engage through their choice of activities and content, and frequently make use of strategies typically emphasised in both constructivist and learner-centred education literatures.*
>
> (Anderson and Taner, 2023, p 1)

This research is based on analysis of 106 empirical studies from 16 countries involving 1124 teachers identified as experts in primary/elementary and secondary contexts from a wide range of educational systems around the world.

In contrast to these large-scale projects, Harper's research (2013) focuses on a much smaller sample, but it is within the FE sector rather than in schools. The purpose of the research was to examine in detail 20 real sessions that were judged to be outstanding and to pin down what, if anything, they had in common and the extent to which the practice observed aligned with any particular pedagogical approach.

The findings concur in many respects with the research cited above. In common with Anderson and Taner, for example, the teaching methods in the FE lessons observed reflect a constructivist approach. The lessons were mostly based on problem-solving and/or authentic tasks, discovery learning, structured discussions and independent study.

The sessions were all planned and managed to focus unashamedly on the genuine development of students' knowledge and skills. Within a highly supportive and inclusive atmosphere, enthusiastic teachers appeared to genuinely want to be in the lesson in order to share their passion and to help their students to learn, enjoy learning and achieve well. It was evident to the students that these dual professionals – including a chef, classicist, social worker and hairdresser – were experts in their subjects as well as in the associated pedagogy. Because of their deep pedagogical content knowledge, they were able to structure very skilfully the unfolding of various concepts and/or practical skills in ways that students found meaningful, challenging and achievable.

7.4 CONTINUING PROFESSIONAL DEVELOPMENT

Continuing professional development (CPD) is the term used to describe the learning activities professionals engage in to keep up to date and to develop and enhance their knowledge and skills.

Many professions require a licence to practise and regular CPD. Anyone who works within a sector that is formally regulated is likely to be required to track and progress their CPD to maintain their licence, for example in healthcare, engineering, construction, accounting and architecture. Professions are regulated by different bodies and the specific requirements for each profession vary. In some cases, CPD is strongly advised and in others it is mandatory. For example, doctors must be registered with the General Medical Council (GMC) in order to practise medicine in the UK. They are expected to carry out

Expertise, professional development and a spot, swot and plot **123**

CPD on an annual basis and to discuss this CPD during appraisal for revalidation every five years. Over this period, they should have completed a minimum of 250 hours.

Task

- If you do not already know, check the licence to practise and CPD requirements for your (non-teaching) profession if you are a dual professional.

Regardless of profession, CPD need not simply be formal training courses or conferences. It can be a combination of approaches and techniques, such as workshops, online portfolios, journal writing, e-learning programmes, visits, placements or informal sharing of ideas. As a dual professional, you may need to consider how to keep up to date both with your specialism and with developments in teaching, learning and assessment. As is noted in the quotation above (Anderson and Taner, 2023) expert teachers are continuous learners throughout their careers.

The CPD ideas for FE teachers described in this chapter may seem daunting if you are still training to teach or have only just recently completed your course. There is no suggestion that you should attempt to undertake all of them.

Professional bodies and subject associations

The Society for Education and Training (SET) is a professional body for teachers, trainers and leaders within the FE sector. Members get access to support, advice, relevant sector research and events.

There are many subject associations for teachers. Even if they are aimed at secondary school or higher education teachers, they may still be useful in terms of keeping in touch with the latest developments. Examples include: the Subject Association for Teachers of Business, Economics and Enterprise (EBEA); the Association of Teachers of Mathematics (ATM); the Institute of Hospitality (IoH); and the Association for the Teaching of Psychology (ATP). Most subject associations are registered charities, and their aims tend to be around the exploration of new ideas; accessing resources and research; providing a platform for teachers to share their expertise; and giving a voice on issues that affect practitioners.

Task

- Find out if there is a subject association for your specialism by asking colleagues and/or searching online. A good starting point is the Council for Subject Associations (CSfA, nd).

Observations of teaching and learning

Many teacher trainees find the observations of experienced teachers to be among the most useful activities in their initial teacher education programme, as well as observations of peers in their group, particularly of those teaching subjects different from their own.

As you move into FE as a qualified teacher, you may experience different types of observations. Gosling (2014) outlines three models of observation: *evaluation*, *developmental* and *collaborative peer review*.

With the evaluation model, senior staff may observe you and provide a report with a judgement, such as a grade or descriptor. This may be linked to a provider's policy in relation to confirming a successful probation, reviewing quality assurance or as part of an annual appraisal scheme.

Developmental observations are usually undertaken by expert or experienced teachers, or advanced practitioners. This might be part of an institution's wider programme to improve teaching generally. The focus here may be on identifying good practice or on how to improve teaching competence. Those observed may be asked to complete an action plan as a consequence of any suggestions made by the observer.

In a collaborative peer review, teachers agree to observe each other and to engage in dialogue about their practice. Participants can choose an aspect they wish to focus on. Unlike the other two models, this is not a judgemental process but an opportunity for constructive debate about teaching, learning and assessment.

Another type of observation is known as a triad. With triad observations, three teachers who work in the same subject area collaborate on planning a lesson. What is important at this stage is the discussion around planning and the rationale for the chosen approach(es). One of the three then teaches the lesson, and one or both of the other two observe. After the lesson, the three colleagues review the lesson together, and their evaluation feeds into the planning of the next session. Next time, they swap roles. Triad observations are recognised as a very powerful form of CPD in the education sector, but the main drawback in an FE setting is time, availability and timetable constraints.

Task

- What do you see as the pros and cons of each of Gosling's three types of observation (evaluation, developmental and collaborative), firstly from a manager's viewpoint and secondly from a teacher's viewpoint?
- What do you consider to be the main benefits of triad observations?

Supported experiments

Supported experiments are normally undertaken as a team. They involve experimenting with an unfamiliar teaching or assessment approach, trying it out several times and then adapting it until it works for the team and more importantly for the students. It can be particularly helpful, for example, with new or unfamiliar technologies. Having access to a new gadget, tool or software program does not necessarily help to improve teaching. Firstly, teachers must learn how to use it, and this might require some technical support. Secondly, teachers need to consider the educational implications, namely, how to use it to enhance students' learning. Other examples of supported experiments might involve trying out something new, such as recording audio or video feedback to students rather than providing written feedback; teaching for a specified period where you only ask questions or even remain silent; or asking second-year students to teach a class for first-year students or to assess one of their assignments. The outcomes of supported experiments can be shared and feed into the practice of others.

Action research

Action research is a form of self-reflective enquiry. The action research cycle begins with a teacher identifying a problem in their practice, such as disaffection among particular students or students having difficulty in understanding particular concepts. The teacher then investigates the problem to gain an understanding of it and then comes up with a solution. The solution is implemented and then evaluated. If the evaluation is positive then the solution might be implemented in practice more widely. If not, the problem might be reframed, and a further action research cycle might begin. An advantage of action research is that it is solution focused and addresses, at least initially, problems in an individual's practice.

Action learning sets

The purpose of an action learning set is to explore and solve problems, drawing on ideas and contributions from other professionals. The sets work best with a group of four or five colleagues, or teachers from different institutions who share a common interest in solving a particular professional problem. The methodology used can vary but one popular approach is to adopt a three-stage process at each meeting, supported by a facilitator. For the first stage, the facilitator invites one participant (the 'presenter') to talk for up to three minutes about a challenge. Others listen but do not speak. At the next stage, the facilitator invites people to ask the presenter one question each. This needs to be an open, rather than closed, question to avoid the possibility of a one-word answer and to encourage the presenter to think more deeply about the problem. The presenter briefly responds to each question. In the final stage, the facilitator invites others to suggest ideas or resources that might help the presenter. The presenter listens and makes notes and these feed into an action plan, which then features in the three-minute presentation at the next session. Each action learning set meeting is planned to ensure that all participants have an opportunity to present their own problem and to hear ideas from others.

Industry placements and engagement with employers

Once you leave a profession, it does not take long before you feel out of touch. For dual professionals working in FE, particularly if teaching on technical courses, an industry placement is an excellent way to update skills and industry knowledge. It may be possible to arrange a placement with a relevant employer, if only for a few days. This type of industry link could be beneficial not just to the teacher, but also to the host organisation if they are looking for apprentices, work placement students or employees. Other types of industry links are valuable too. Examples include arranging for employers to provide resources such as real case studies for student assignments, give presentations to students, host on-site visits or contribute towards curriculum design. These activities are not just beneficial for students and employers but can also contribute to your own CPD.

Informal learning, team teaching, shadowing others and 'TeachMeets'

Supported experiments, action research, action learning sets and industry placements are formal in that they have to be organised in advance. Teachers often find they learn best from each other informally. Valuable exchanges of ideas often take place by chance in the staff room, canteen or corridor or by the photocopier.

A less formal activity that can be arranged easily is team teaching, which can be very helpful, particularly with a more experienced teacher. The way in which a colleague plans the lesson, assesses learning or manages the group may be very different to your own approach and this might provide ideas for future sessions.

A TeachMeet is an organised but informal meeting often held at the end of the day or at lunchtime on a weekly, monthly or termly basis. The purpose is partly social but also to share good practice and innovations.

Work shadowing is another form of CPD, whereby you follow a member of staff for the whole day, in and out of the classroom, in order to get a sense of their job. It may also be possible to follow a group of students for the day as they go to different lessons. What is fascinating about this particular activity is seeing the same students with different teachers. It reinforces the fact that what a teacher does or does not do makes a difference. For example, if the students are particularly hard-working, engaged and well behaved with one teacher but not with the others, what is it about this teacher's practice that has such a positive impact on the students? It may be difficult for a trainee or new teacher observing this experienced teacher to articulate what makes it works so well, as expert teachers, as noted earlier, make their practice look very easy and effortless.

Mentoring and coaching

New teachers are often allocated a mentor in their first year. The role of the mentor is to share their knowledge, skills and experience and offer advice to help the mentee's professional development. The mentor is not your line manager and should be able to offer honest and constructive feedback and also maintain confidentiality. The terms *mentor* and *coach* are sometimes used interchangeably, but the role of a coach is different in that the focus is on helping the new teacher to think and to work out solutions to problems for themselves.

Reading, writing, listening and watching

CPD may focus on reading material about your profession and your practice, listening to podcasts or watching relevant clips online. You may also engage in writing anything, from your own reflective journal to articles for publication. When you undertake your own research and prepare resources for your lessons, this too is a form of CPD.

Moderation, examining, marking and inspection

Once settled into teaching, some teachers choose to become verifiers, moderators, external markers or part-time inspectors. This helps them to understand external requirements, to further develop their knowledge and skills, and to share what they learn from this experience with colleagues, and it also benefits their students.

Formal activities: conferences, staff development and further study

CPD is often associated with participation at conferences and at staff development events, or with further qualifications, such as a master's or a doctorate, involving research. As a new teacher, you are likely to be attending various events as a guest, but as you gain more experience you may find yourself presenting the findings of your own research at conferences and staff development events.

Mandatory training

While there is considerable freedom around the CPD activities you choose to undertake, in almost all FE providers there are is also some mandatory training. This might include, for example, annual updates on the institution's safeguarding, data protection or cyber-security policies.

Task

- From the list of professional development activities, which appeal most to you?
- Why?

7.5 SPOT, SWOT AND PLOT

The three tasks in this section provide an opportunity to think about your own professional development. The first is *spot* (select a topic); the second is *swot* (identify strengths, weakness, opportunities and threats); and the third is *plot* (draw up an action plan).

The way in which you complete these tasks is up to you. The task requires you choose one topic, but you may wish to select more than one. Included are tables with examples, but rather than type or write these you may prefer to record audio or video versions. Alternatively, you may want to use an electronic project planning tool for the action plan in the last of the three activities. This activity could be used as a starting point for a discussion with your tutor or workplace mentor. Whichever approach you take, what is important is that the spotting, swotting and plotting leads to meaningful reflection and planning.

Before undertaking the tasks, you will need to familiarise yourself with the areas of knowledge and understanding, professional values, skills and behaviours common to the occupational duties (OD) of the apprenticeship and the Education and Training Foundation's Professional Standards (PS). These are:

1. promote a passion for learning and have high expectations (OD1, PS3);
2. demonstrate, maintain and evidence excellent pedagogy, subject, curriculum and industry knowledge and practice and research (OD3, PS8);
3. model professional, collaborative and respectful relationships with students, colleagues and stakeholders (OD6, PS6);
4. understand your teaching role and responsibilities and how these are influenced by legal, regulatory, institutional and ethical contexts (OD7, PS12);
5. select and use digital technologies safely and effectively to promote learning (OD4, PS16);
6. apply appropriate and fair methods of assessment and provide constructive and timely feedback to support learning and achievement (OD4, PS19);
7. value and champion diversity, equal opportunity, inclusion and social equity (OD5, PS5);
8. promote education for sustainable development (OD8, PS2);
9. provide access to up-to-date information, advice and guidance so that learners can take ownership of their learning and make informed progression choices and collaborate with employers, higher education and/or community groups (OD2, PS18).

Task

Spot

- Select a topic from the list above that is of particular relevance to your current teaching role or to a role you may adopt in the future.
- Identify in which chapter(s) the topic appears, as in the example in Table 7.1.

Swot

- Using the topic you selected for the previous task, revisit the relevant chapters and then assess the strengths, weaknesses, opportunities and threats to your practice, as in the example given in Table 7.2.

Plot

- Based on the swot, draw up an action plan, as in the example in Table 7.3.

Table 7.1 Spot example

Apply appropriate and fair methods of assessment and provide constructive and timely feedback to support learning and achievement (OD4, PS19). (Area 6 of knowledge and understanding, professional values, skills and behaviours.)	
Assessment for learning	Chapter 3
Reliability of assessment	Chapter 4
Range of assessment strategies	Chapter 4
Peer assessment	Chapter 4
Quality assurance of assessment	Chapter 4
Differentiation in assessment	Chapter 5
Sustainable assessment	Chapter 6

Table 7.2 Swot example

Spotlight issues	Strengths	Weaknesses	Opportunities	Threats
Assessment for learning (AfL)	My feedback on written work is very detailed.	Is my written feedback too detailed? In my questioning, I may often supply an answer instead of being patient.	Ask colleagues about my written feedback during moderation/internal verification. Self-video a lesson/ask for an observation/coaching session.	Re written feedback –students may be demotivated by detail. Not using AfL enough to plan future sessions.
Reliability of assessment		Do I have preconceived ideas about student ability and achievement when marking work?	Experiment with blind marking?	Difficult to assess individual progress with blind marking.
Range of assessment strategies		I use a limited range of assessment strategies.	Use constructive alignment to devise more appropriate assessment strategies.	Students feel safer with more traditional assessment strategies.
Peer assessment	Peers honest with one another.	Are peers experienced enough to give informed feedback?	Use peer assessment but monitor carefully.	Students do not take it seriously enough.
Quality assurance of assessment		Uncertain about awarding organisation assessment standards.	Apply to be an external verifier.	Will I find the time to do this properly?

Spotlight issues	Strengths	Weaknesses	Opportunities	Threats
Differentiation in assessment		Find it challenging to practically manage differentiated assessment strategies with different students in the same session.	Ask colleagues or mentor.	Weaker students make less progress.
Sustainable assessment		Students have problems identifying and relating sustainability issues across their learning programmes.	Devise synoptic assessments which require relating issues across modules.	Students do not value the importance of sustainability.

Table 7.3 Plot example

Spotlight issues	Proposed actions	Responsibility for actions	Intended targets/ outcomes	Timings
Assessment for learning (AfL)	Ask colleagues about my written feedback during moderation. Ask students if they understand the feedback. Self-video/ coaching session. Use AfL for planning future sessions.	Self and colleagues. Self. Self and mentor.	Reach more of a balance in detail or change marking strategy–annotation of text rather than summative marking? Feedback more formative.	End of module at end of term.
Reliability of assessment	Experiment with blind marking.	Self.	More objective assessment judgements.	End of module at end of term.
Range of assessment strategies	Use constructive alignment in session planning to devise more appropriate assessment strategies.	Self.	Greater fairness in assessment.	Currently planning next week's sessions.
Peer assessment	Use more peer assessment but monitor carefully.	Self.	Students' deeper learning.	Plan into next week's sessions.
Quality assurance of assessment	Apply to be an external verifier.	Self with line manager support.	Deeper understanding of QA.	For September.

Spotlight issues	Proposed actions	Responsibility for actions	Intended targets/ outcomes	Timings
Differentiation in assessment	Observation of experienced colleagues.	Self and colleagues.	More effectively managed differentiated assessment strategies.	As soon as can be arranged.
Sustainable assessment	Devise synoptic assessments which require relating issues across modules.	Self and colleagues.	Students' better understanding of issues.	Next team meeting.

7.6 NEXT STAGES

Looking to the future, the status of Qualified Teacher Learning and Skills (QTLS) is available for teachers who have successfully completed their initial training. This can be gained after completing a period of 'professional formation' and maintained through membership of the Society for Education and Training (SET). The professional formation involves a self-guided online portfolio demonstrating how, since gaining your initial teacher training qualification, you have continued to develop your values, knowledge and skills. Achieving QTLS allows you to teach in schools on the same terms as teachers with Qualified Teacher Status (QTS).

As outlined by SET (2023), looking ahead, Advanced Teacher Status (ATS) offers a stage beyond QTLS to recognise advanced teachers and trainers with significant experience, who can demonstrate, at a high level, mastery in three major competencies: continuing self-improvement and development of pedagogical practice and subject specialism; commitment to the development of others through coaching and mentoring activity with colleagues; and ability to influence internal and external stakeholders and effect change in curriculum, and improve organisational quality and development.

7.7 CONCLUSION

As a teacher in FE you are improving life chances for both young people and older learners. As such, the book provides a starting point for discussion about the topics that matter to those who teach in FE – teaching, learning and assessment, inclusion, diversity and well-being, sustainable education and professional development. The references to TV programmes provide an unusual lens through which to discuss these topics but should help to provoke debate and create opportunities to reflect on your own practice. Reflective practice is the ability to reflect on one's actions so as to engage in the process of continuous learning (Schön, 1991). How you approach this learning and how you choose to reflect is very personal and will not be the same for all teachers. There is no one 'correct' way, as so much will depend on your own preference, experience and context, but the book is here to provide food for thought.

REFERENCES

Anderson, J and Taner, G (2023) Building the Expert Teacher Prototype: A Metasummary of Teacher Expertise Studies in Primary and Secondary Education. *Educational Research Review*, 38.

Coe, R, Aloisi, C, Higgins, S and Elliot Major, L (2014) *What Makes Great Teaching? Review of the Underpinning Research.* The Sutton Trust. [online] Available at: www.suttontrust.com/wp-content/uploads/2014/10/What-Makes-Great-Teaching-REPORT.pdf (accessed 11 February 2024).

Council for Subject Associations (CSfA) (nd) [online] Available at: www.subjectassociations.org.uk (accessed 11 February 2024).

Dreyfus, H L and Dreyfus, S E (1986) *Mind Over Machine.* Oxford: Basil Blackwell.

Education and Training Foundation (2022) *Professional Standards for Teachers and Trainers in the Further Education and Training Sector: Guide to Using the Updated 2022 Professional Standards.* London: ETF. [online] Available at: www.et-foundation.co.uk/wp-content/uploads/2022/06/PS-for-Teachers_Guide-to-Using-the-Updated-2022-Professional-Standards_Final.pdf (accessed 11 February 2024).

Gosling, D (2014) Collaborative Peer-Supported Review of Teaching. In Sachs, J and Parsell, M (eds) *Peer Review of Learning and Teaching in Higher Education* (pp 13–32). Dordrecht: Springer.

Harper, H (2013) *Outstanding Teaching in Lifelong Learning.* Maidenhead: McGraw-Hill Education/Open University Press.

Hattie, J A C (1999) *Influences on Student Learning.* Inaugural Professorial Address, University of Auckland, New Zealand. [online] Available at: www.researchgate.net/publication/237248564_Influences_on_Student_Learning (accessed 11 February 2024).

Hattie, J A C (2003) Teachers Make a Difference: What is the Research Evidence? Paper presented at *Building Teacher Quality: What Does the Research Tell Us?* ACER Research Conference, Melbourne, Australia, October 2003. [online] Available at: http://research.acer.edu.au/research_conference_2003/4/ (accessed 11 February 2024).

Korthagen, F (2004) In Search of the Essence of a Good Teacher: Towards a More Holistic Approach. *Teaching and Teacher Education*, 20: 77–97.

Saner, E (2022) A New Start After 60: 'I Won MasterChef – and Finally Learned to Believe in Myself'. *The Guardian*, 18 April. [online] Available at: www.theguardian.com/lifeandstyle/2022/apr/18/a-new-start-after-60-masterchef-believe-in-myself-irini-tzortzoglou-chef-speaker (accessed 11 February 2024).

Schön, D (1983, 1991 edition) *The Reflective Practitioner: How Professionals Think in Action.* Aldershot: Ashgate Publishing Ltd.

Society for Education and Training (SET) (2023) QTLS – Qualified Teacher Learning and Skills Status. [online] Available at: https://set.et-foundation.co.uk/your-career/qtls (accessed 11 February 2024).

TV programmes

Big Dreams, Small Spaces	BBC TV
Bill Nye Saves the World	Netflix
Blue Planet II	BBC TV
Britain's Got Talent	ITVX
Castaway 2000	Lion TV for BBC TV
Celebrity Dancing on Ice	Lifted Entertainment for ITV
Celebrity MasterChef	BBC TV
Celebrity Race Across the World	BBC TV
Celebrity Tipping Point	ITVX
Cooked	Netflix
Cowspiracy: The Sustainability Secret	Netflix
Dancing on Ice	Lifted Entertainment for ITV
DIY SOS: The Big Build	BBC TV
Dragons' Den	BBC Studios for BBC TV
Eurovision Song Contest	European Broadcasting Union
Freeze the Fear with Wim Hof	BBC TV
Frozen Planet II	BBC TV
Garden Rescue	BBC TV
Glow Up: Britain's Next Make-Up Star	BBC TV
Gogglebox	Studio Lambert for Channel 4
Great British Menu	Optomen for BBC TV
Ground Force	BBC TV
I'm a Celebrity... Get Me Out of Here!	ITV
Interior Design Masters	BBC TV
Jamie's Kitchen	Talkback Productions for Channel 4
Love Island	ITV
Made in Chelsea	Monkey Television for Channel 4
MasterChef	BBC TV
MasterChef: The Professionals	BBC TV
Mastermind	BBC TV
On the Buses	ITV
Only Connect	RDF Television for BBC TV
Our Planet	Netflix
Planet Earth	BBC TV
QI	Talkback Productions for BBC TV
Race Across the World	Studio Lambert for BBC TV
RuPaul's Drag Race	MTV
Strictly Come Dancing	BBC Studios for BBC TV
Supernanny	Ricochet South for Channel 4

The Age of Consequences	PF Pictures
The Apprentice	MGM Television for BBC TV
The Benny Hill Show	BBC TV
The Chase	ITV
The Dog Academy	Five Mile Films for Channel 4
The Great British Bake Off	Love Productions for Channel 4
The Great British Sewing Bee	Love Productions for BBC TV
The Great Celebrity Bake Off	Love Productions for Channel 4
The Great Pottery Throwdown	Love Productions for BBC TV
The Only Way Is Essex	Lime Pictures for ITV
The Repair Shop	Ricochet for BBC TV
The Story of Stuff	Free Range Studios
The Undateables	Betty for Channel 4
The Voice	ITVX
The X Factor	ITV
Tipping Point	ITV
Traitors	BBC TV
Ultimate Wedding Planner	BBC TV
University Challenge	Lifted Entertainment for BBC TV
Waste Not	National Geographic
Who Wants to Be a Millionaire?	Stellify Media/Sony Pictures Television for ITV
Who Wants to Be a Millionaire? Celebrity Special	ITV
Years of Living Dangerously	Showtime/National Geographic
Your Home Made Perfect	BBC TV

Index

Page numbers in *italics* and **bold** refer to figures and tables, respectively.

academic tutorials, 47
action learning sets, 125
action research, 125
active listening, 48
adult community education providers, 6
Age of Consequences, The, 111
age stereotypes, 84–5
Apprentice, The, 24, **24**, 25, 45, 112
apprenticeships, 9, 22, 83
assessment
  active strategies, 67–70
  authenticity of, 60
  criterion and grade referencing, 58
  criterion referencing, 58
  evidence-based, 71–3
  extended, 73–4
  fairness in, 65–6, 70
  features of, 56
  grade referencing, 57–8
  initial, 54, 63–5
  ipsative referencing, 59
  of learning process, 56
  moderation process, 74
  norm referencing, 57
  peer assessment, 70–1
  planning of, 61–3
  practicability of, 60
  of product of learning, 56
  purposes of, 54–5
  quality assurance of, 74–5
  reliability of, 59–60
  self-assessment, 70–1
  standardization process, 74
  tests and challenges, **68**
  tests and challenges strategies, 65–6
  validity of, 59
  yardstick, 56–9
assessment for learning (AfL), 43–4
Association for the Teaching of Psychology (ATP), 123
Association of Teachers of Mathematics (ATM), 123
augmented reality (AR), 23
autonomy, 71

behaviourism, 28–9
Benny Hill Show, The, 82
Big Dreams, Small Spaces, 39, 48, 102
Bill Nye Saves the World, 111
blended learning, 23
Blue Planet II, 111
Britain's Got Talent, 79
broadcasting, 2

Carry On films, 82, 87
Castaway 2000, 30
Celebrity Bake Off, 118
Celebrity Dancing on Ice, 4
Celebrity MasterChef, 4, 78, 118
celebrity version of shows, 4
Celebrity Who Wants to be a Millionaire?, 4
Chase, The, 18
coaching, 48, 126
collaborative learning, 45–6
collaborative peer review, 124
communities of practice, 30–1
competitiveness, 31
constructive alignment, 42, 61
constructivism, 30, 46
continuing professional development (CPD), 122–3
  action learning sets, 125
  action research, 125
  formal activities, 127
  industry placements and engagement with employers, 125–6
  informal learning, 126
  mandatory training, 127
  mentoring and coaching, 126
  moderation, examining, marking, inspection practice, 127
  observations of teaching and learning, 124
  professional bodies and subject associations, 123
  reading, writing, listening, watching practice, 126
  supported experiments, 124–5
  TeachMeets, 126
  work shadowing, 126
continuous assessment, 56
Cooked, 111

Cowspiracy: The Sustainability Secret, 111
criterion and grade referencing, 58
criterion referencing, 58
critical pedagogy, 41
critical thinking skills, 90
cultivation theory, 2
culture, 82
curriculum
   combined model, 101
   concurrent model, 100
   consecutive model, 100
   content model, 99
   models, 99–100
   process model, 99
   product model, 99–100
   reform, 10–12
   situational model, 99
   structures, 100–1
   technology in, 50–1

Dancing on Ice, 18, 25, 47, 58, 78, 83, 102, 103
Dean, Christopher, 36
deep learning, 32
developmental observations, 124
digital poverty, 85
digital tools, 51–2
Dimmock, Charlie, 36
disability, 77–80
diversity, 81–2
   age, 84–5
   gender, 82–3
   intersectionality, 85–6
   language, 86–8
   race and culture, 82
   sexuality, 83
   social class, 84
DIY SOS: The Big Build, 46, 73
Dog Academy, The, 28, 29
Don, Monty, 39
Dragons' Den, 46, 49, 68, 69
dual professionals, 37, 116
duties, 116–17

education for sustainable development (ESD), 97–8, 103–5
effective teaching, 121
employers, engagement with, 125–6
English for speakers of other languages (ESOL), 9
English skill, 49–50
Eurovision Song Contest, 58
evaluation model, of observation, 124
evidence-based assessment, 71–3
expectancy theory, 33
expertise development
   expert teacher, 120–2
   skill acquisition, 117–20
extended assessment, 73–4
extrinsic motivation, 31–2

fixed mindset, **33**, 81
formal assessment, 56
formative assessment, 56
free school meals (FSM), 84
Freeze the Fear with Wim Hof, 32
Frozen Planet II, 51, 52
further education (FE)
   academic qualifications, 10
   adult provisions, 9
   apprenticeships, 9
   curriculum reform, 10–12
   full-time provision for younger students, 9
   GCSEs, 9–10
   learning skills in, 19
   providers, 5–7
   qualifications and curricula, 7–8
   vocational/technical qualifications, 9
fusion skills, 108–9

Galetti, Monica, 36
Garden Rescue, 25
GCSEs, 9–10
gender, 82–3
general further education (GFE) colleges, 5–6
genres, **15**
Gerbner, George, 2
Glow Up: Britain's Next Make-Up Star, 42, 57
Gogglebox, 30
grade referencing, 57–8
Great British Bake Off, The, 18, 20, 32, 45, 48, **50**, 56, 57, 71, 81, 82, 117
Great British Menu, 70, 71
Great British Sewing Bee, The, 18, 20, 117
Great Expectations, 30
Great Pottery Throw Down, The, 18, 22, 57, 117, 118
green skills, 106–8
Ground Force, 39
group learning, 23–5
growth mindset, **33**
Guru-Murthy, Krishnan, 2

heritage craft skills, 105–6
Honey and Mumford model, 27
Horrex, Wendy, 3
hybrid learning, 52

I'm a Celebrity ... Get Me Out of Here!, 4, 78
inclusion, 77
   and disability, 77–80
   inclusive teaching, 80–1, 90
   neurodiversity, 81
income sources for FE, 6
independent learning, 44–5
independent training/learning providers, 6
industry placements, 101–2, 125–6
informal assessment, 56
informal learning, 126
Institute of Hospitality (IoH), 123
Interior Design Masters, 57
International Baccalaureate (IB), 10
intersectionality, 85–6
intrinsic motivation, 31–2
ipsative referencing, 59

Jamie's Kitchen, 32

knowledge, 18, 19
Kolb's experiential learning cycle, 26, 26, 120

language diversity, 86–8
learning
   apprenticeships, 22
   augmented and virtual realities, 23
   blended learning, 23
   group learning, 23–5
   motivations for, 31–4
   from observation, 21–2
   one-to-one training, 23
   outcomes, 42
   and practice, 25
   and reflective practice, 25–6
   styles, 27
learning difficulties and/or disabilities (LDD), 77–80
learning theories, 26–7
   behaviourism, 28–9
   communities of practice, 30–1
   constructivism, 30, 46
   neuroscience, 27
Leith, John, 2
Love Island, 4, 5

Mabuse, Oti, 47
Made in Chelsea, 84
MasterChef, 18, 20, 22, 24, 55, 57, 63–5, 71, 117, 118
MasterChef: The Professionals, 63
Mastermind, 18, 50, 65
mathematics skill, 49–50
mentoring, 126
mindsets, 33–4, **33**, 81

moderation
   and assessment, 74
   and CPD, 127

National Numeracy, 20
negative emotions, 27
neurodiversity, 81
neuroscience, 27
norm referencing, 57

objective assessment, 56
observations
   learning from, 21–2
   of teaching and learning, 124
On the Buses, 82
one-to-one teaching, 47
one-to-one training, 23
Only Connect, 24
Only Way is Essex, The, 84
Open University, 21
Our Planet, 96, 110
Outliers, 25

pastoral tutorials, 47
Pavlov, Ivan, 28
pedagogical content knowledge (PCK), 41
pedagogy
   critical, 41
   generic, 39–40
   subject-specific, 40–1
   vocational, 40
peer assessment, 70–1
Planet Earth, 96, 111
plot task, 127–31
popular TV, 2
positive emotions, 27
practice
   communities of, 30–1
   significance of, 25
prison education, 6
Professional Practice module, assessment of, 71–3
professional standards, 117
Professional Standards for Teachers and Trainers, 15, 37, 117
professional tutorials, 47
professionalism, 36, 116
   dual professionals, 37
   professional standards, 37

QI, 50

race, 82
Race Across the World, 65, 67, 68

reality TV, 2
  as mediated reality, 4
  and socio-politics, 4–5
reflective practice, 25–6, 131
Regulated Qualifications Framework for England, Wales and Northern Ireland, **7–8**
Repair Café, The, 106
Repair Shop, The, 105
resourcing, 1
Richard Review, 11
robots, 52
role reversal, 90
RuPaul's Drag Race, 57

scheme of work (SOW), 111
self-assessment, 70–1
self-care, 91–2
self-learning, reasons for, 22
SEND (special educational needs and disability), 77
sexism, 82
sexuality, 83
skill acquisition, 117–19, 120
  advanced beginner stage, 119
  competent stage, 119
  expertise stage, 119
  novice stage, 119
  proficient stage, 119
skills, 18–19
  learning. *See* learning
  learning skills in the FE sector, 19
  threshold concepts, 20
  threshold skills, 20–1
Skills for Jobs: Lifelong Learning for Opportunity and Growth (2021), 11
Skinner, B F, 28
social class, 84
Society for Education and Training (SET), 123, 131
specialism, 118
spot task, 127–31
SquareMeal, 55
staff
  significance of, 13–15
  well-being of, 91–2
standardization, and assessment, 74
Story of Stuff, The, 111
storytelling, importance of, 3
strategic learning, 33
stress-reduction approaches, 92
Strictly Come Dancing, 1, 2, 18, 23, 25, 32, 47, 58, 59, 77, 82, 83, 85, 102, 103, 117
structured reality, 84
students, significance of, 12–13
students' skills, development of, 44
  collaborative learning, 45–6
  independent learning, 44–5

Subject Association for Teachers of Business, Economics and Enterprise (EBEA), 123
subjective assessment, 56
subject-specific pedagogy, 40–1
summative assessment, 56
Supernanny, 28–9
supported experiments, 124–5
surface learning, 32
sustainability
  education for sustainable development (ESD), 97–8
  individual lessons/sessions, 112–13
  overview, 112
  sequence/structure, 112
  teaching and learning activities for, 109–10
  and TV programmes, 110–11
sustainability in jobs and skills
  fusion skills, 108–9
  green skills, 106–8
  heritage craft skills, 105–6
sustainable curriculum
  curriculum models, 99–100
  curriculum structures, 100–1
  education for sustainable development (ESD), 103–5
  industry placements, 101–2
  resources, 103
  universal design for learning (UDL), 102–3
sustainable development, 95–6
Sustainable Development Goals (SDGs), 96
sustainable organisation, 96–7
swot task, 127–31

teaching
  assessment for learning (AfL), 43–4
  effective, 121
  expertise, 120–2
  inclusive, 80–1, 90
  and learning outcomes, 42
  methods, 43, **43**
  one-to-one, 47
  pedagogy, 39–41
  professionalism, 36–7
  and students' skill development, 44–6
  teachers, role of, 39
  and technology, 50–2
  tutorials, 47–8
TeachMeets, 126
technology
  assistive, 79–80
  in the curriculum, 50–1
  digital tools, 51–2
terminal assessment, 56
tests and challenges, assessment strategies, 65–6
text-to-voice application, 79–80

theory, 48–9
threshold concepts, 20
threshold skills, 20–1
Tipping Point, 65
Tomlinson Report, 11
Torvill, Jayne, 36
triad observations, 124
tutorials, 47–8

Ultimate Wedding Planner, The, 112, 113
Undateables, The, 5
universal design for learning (UDL), 102–3
University Challenge, 18, 24, 50, 65, 69, 70

VARK model, 27
virtual reality (VR), 23, 52
vocational pedagogy, 40
Voice, The, 47, 102, 103

Waste Not, 110
well-being, 88
    of staff, 91–2
    of students, 88–91
What? So What? Now What?, 26
Who Wants to be a Millionaire?, 18, 65
Wolf Report, 11
work shadowing, 126
workforce, 13–15

X (formerly Twitter), 2

Years of Living Dangerously, 111
Your Home Made Perfect, 51
YouTube, 22

zone of proximal development (ZPD), 19

Milton Keynes UK
Ingram Content Group UK Ltd.
UKHW051955220424
441555UK00002B/3